Authentication Systems
for Secure Networks

The Artech House Computer Science Library

ATM Switching Systems, Thomas M. Chen and Stephen S. Liu
  ISBN: 0-89006-682-5

Authentication Systems for Secure Networks, Rolf Oppliger
  ISBN: 0-89006-510-1

Client/Server Computing: Architecture, Applications, and Distributed Sytems Management, Bruce Elbert and Bobby Martyna ISBN: 0-89006-691-4

Computer-Mediated Communications: Multimedia Applications,
  Rob Walters ISBN: 0-89006-757-0

Computer Telephone Integration, Rob Walters ISBN: 0-89006-660-4

Distributed and Multi-Database Systems, Angelo R. Bobak
  ISBN: 0-89006-614-0

A Guide to Programming Languages: Overview and Comparison,
  Ruknet Cezzar ISBN: 0-89006-812-7

Introduction to Document Image Processing Techniques,
  Ronald G. Matteson ISBN: 0-89006-492-X

Managing Computer Networks: A Case-Based Reasoning Approach, Lundy
  Lewis ISBN: 0-89006-799-6

Networks and Imaging Systems in a Windowed Environment, Marc R.
  D'Alleyrand ISBN: 0-89006-654-X

Survival in the Software Jungle, Mark Norris ISBN: 0-89006-831-3

UNIX Internetworking, Second Edition, Uday O. Pabrai
  ISBN: 0-89006-778-3

Wireless LAN Systems, A. Santamaría and F. J. López-Hernández
  ISBN: 0-89006-609-4

Wireless: The Revolution in Personal Telecommunications, Ira Brodsky
  ISBN: 0-89006-717-1

X Window System User's Guide, Uday O. Pabrai
  ISBN: 0-89006-740-6

For further information on these and other Artech House titles, contact:

Artech House
685 Canton Street
Norwood, MA 01602
617-769-9750
Fax: 617-762-9230
Telex: 951-659
email: artech@world.std.com

Artech House
Portland House, Stag Place
London SW1E 5XA England
+44 (0) 171-973-8077
Fax: +44 (0)171-630-0166
Telex: 951-659
email: bookco@artech.demon.co.uk

Authentication Systems for Secure Networks

Rolf Oppliger

Artech House
Boston • London

Library of Congress Cataloguing-in-Publication Data
Oppliger, Rolf.
  Authentication systems for secure networks / Rolf Oppliger.
    p.   cm.
  Includes bibliographical references and index.
  ISBN 0-89006-510-1 (alk. paper)
  1. Computer networks–Security measures. 2. Computers–Access control.
3. Authentication. 4. Cryptography.   I. Title.
TK5105.59.O77 1996
005.8–dc20   95-53773
                                                       CIP

British Library Cataloguing in Publication Data
Oppliger, Rolf
  Authentication systems for secure networks
1. Computer networks–Security measures
I. Title
005.8

ISBN 0-89006-510-1

© 1996 ARTECH HOUSE, INC.
685 Canton Street
Norwood, MA 02062

International Standard Book Number: 0-89006-510-1
Library of Congress Catalog Card Number: 95-53773

10 9 8 7 6 5 4 3 2 1

To Isabelle, in memory of our stay in Berkeley

Contents

Preface

Everything should be made
as simple as possible, but not simpler.

— Albert Einstein

When I entered the field of cryptology and information security, the situation was somehow strange. Almost everyone agreed that the data encryption standard (DES) had come to its end and that it needed to be replaced, but nobody knew with what to actually replace it. The very few encryption algorithms that were available at that time hadn't won their spurs yet.

When I later moved to the field of authentication and key distribution in computer networks and distributed systems, the situation looked similar to me. Again, there was one dominant system, namely the Kerberos authentication and key distribution system developed at the Massachusetts Institute of Technology (MIT), and again there was the claim to push the system from its throne without having a viable alternative readily available.

In this situation, I was tasked to evaluate the currently available authentication and key distribution systems. The task was expected to become difficult, mainly because it led into the mysterious field of cryptology and cryptographic protocols. Indeed, the task did turn out to be difficult. However, the astonishing fact was that the task didn't turn out to be difficult because of the intrinsic difficulty of cryptographic protocols, but because of the different ideas and design philosophies that underlay the protocols as well as the different terminologies and notations that are used to describe them. If I hadn't known that the authentication and key distribution systems that implement these protocols in fact try to solve the very same problem(s), I probably wouldn't have guessed so; at least not at first sight.

This book, *Authentication Systems for Secure Networks*, has evolved from the pain and frustration that I suffered during the evaluation of the currently available authentication and key distribution systems. The pain was caused by the need to work my way through a huge stack of technical documents and specifications, and frustration was caused by the fact that at the very end I had to realize that all systems could have been simplified to a certain degree, if only the same terminology and notation would have been used to describe them. At this point, I decided to write this book, and to let its readers participate in my experience.

In accordance with Einstein's quotation that introduces this book, I have tried to simplify as much as possible, but not more. The book goes beyond the information that is usually found in introductory books on network security, technical documents, and specifications. It does not only describe how the various authentication and key distribution systems work, but also seeks to explain the fundamental key decisions that have actually led to the current design.

This book is not tutorial in nature. It assumes the reader to be familiar with the fundamentals of computer networks and distributed systems, as well as cryptology and the use of cryptographic protocols in networked and distributed environments. This is quite a lot, I know. However, I (still) believe that the assumption is realistic, given the fact that anybody who is not familiar with these topics is probably not interested in authentication and key distribution at all. Many of the references cited throughout the book are tutorial and may be used to obtain any background information required. With regard to computer networks and distributed systems, I recommend (Comer, 1988; Tanenbaum, 1988; Carl-Mitchell and Quaterman, 1993; Piscitello and Chapin, 1993). With regard to cryptology in general, I recommend (Konheim, 1981; Meyer and Matias, 1982; Denning, 1982; Brassard, 1988; Schneier, 1994; Rhee, 1994; Stinson, 1995), and with regard to the use of cryptographic protocols in networked and distributed environments, I recommend (Muftic, 1989; Muftic et al., 1993; Purser, 1993; Ford, 1994; Stallings, 1994; Kaufman, Perlman, and Speciner, 1995). Historical notes on cryptology and cryptographic protocols can be found in (Kahn, 1967; Kahn, 1991), and a good source for contemporary information are the frequently asked questions (FAQ) that are periodically posted to the corresponding USENET newsgroups.

The general structure of this book is to focus on one particular authentication and key distribution system in every single chapter, and to summarize its development, overview its architecture, and describe and discuss the cryptographic protocols that it implements in separate sections. However, the characteristics of particular authentication and key distribution systems have urged me to diverge from this general structure occasionally.

The book currently consists of nine chapters, one appendix, a glossary, and a list of abbreviations and acronyms:

- Chapter 1 gives reasons for the use of authentication and key distribution systems in networked and distributed environments.

- Chapter 2 describes and discusses the authentication and key distribution system Kerberos developed at the Massachusetts Institute of Technology (MIT). With respect to its popularity within the Internet community, Kerberos is notably the starting point to discuss authentication and key distribution in computer networks and distributed systems.

- Chapter 3 describes and discusses the authentication and key distribution system NetSP developed by the International Business Machines Corporation (IBM). The distinguishing feature of NetSP is its use of a keyed one-way hash function instead of a full-fledged cryptosystem.

- Chapter 4 describes and discusses the authentication and key distribution system SPX developed and prototyped by the Digital Equipment Corporation (DEC). SPX was historically the first authentication and key distribution system that followed a hybrid approach, and consequently combined the use of secret and public key cryptography.

- Chapter 5 describes and discusses The Exponential Security System (TESS), which is a toolbox-set security system of different but cooperating cryptographic mechanisms and functions based on the primitive of discrete exponentiation.

- Chapter 6 focuses on the European research and development project SESAME that has extended the basic Kerberos model to additionally provide authorization and access control services.

- Chapter 7 describes and discusses the Open Software Foundation's distributed computing environment (OSF DCE) in general, and the OSF DCE security service in particular. Similar to SESAME, the OSF DCE security service also extends the basic Kerberos model to additionally provide authorization and access control services.

- Chapter 8 compares the authentication and key distribution systems that have been described and discussed in the previous chapters of this book.

- Chapter 9 concludes with an epilog and some remarks on Internet security.

- Appendix A summarizes the generic security service application programming interface (GSS-API) that most authentication and key distribution systems conform to.

- The glossary defines the most important terms that are used in this book.

- The abbreviations and acronyms compiles a list of abbreviations and acronyms that are used in this book.

The references that are related to particular authentication and key distribution systems are enumerated, put in square brackets, and appended to the corresponding chapters, whereas the citations that are of general interest are listed in alphabetical order in a Bibliography towards the end of the book. With regard to both of them, namely the lists of references and the bibliography, I have taken great care to be complete and up to date.

Whenever possible, I have also appended some uniform resource locators (URLs) as footnotes to the text. The URLs point to corresponding information pages provided within the World Wide Web (WWW). With respect to these URLs, I apologize for any information page that may have been removed or replaced since my last try during the writing of this book. The WWW has turned out to be very dynamic, and there is good and bad about this, too. One bad thing is notably that URLs tend to point to nowhere after a certain amount of time.

At the end of the book, I have appended an about the author page to tell you a little bit about me, and an index to help you find particular terms.

Because of the nature of this book, it is necessary to mention some company, product, and service names. However, it is only fair to mention that the presence or absence of a specific name neither implies any criticism or endorsement, nor does it imply that the corresponding company, product, or service is necessarily the best available. The following list summarizes the trademarks that appear throughout the book. Note that the list is not comprehensive, and that other trademarks may appear throughout the book, too.

AIX and OS/2	are registered trademarks of International Business Machines Corporation (IBM).
Kerberos	is a trademark of the Massachusetts Institute of Technology (MIT).
NetSP and RACF	are trademarks of International Business Machines Corporation (IBM).
Notes	is a trademark of Lotus Development Corporation.
S/KEY	is a trademark of Bellcore.
UNIX	is a registered trademark in the United States and other countries, licensed exclusively through X/Open Company Ltd.
DOS, Windows and Windows NT	are trademarks of Microsoft Corporation.
X/Open	is a trademark of X/Open Company Ltd.

I would like to take the opportunity to invite you as a reader of this book to let me know your opinions and thoughts. If you have something to correct or add, please let me know. If I haven't expressed myself clearly, or if I have even obscured things, please let me know, too. I appreciate and welcome any comment or suggestion, in order to update the book periodically. I can be reached by e-mail at `oppliger@iam.unibe.ch` or `rolf.oppliger@bfi.admin.ch`. You can also contact my home page on the WWW by following the URL `http://iamwww.unibe.ch/~oppliger`.

Acknowledgments

An old proverb says that an author is necessary but not sufficient to write and publish a book. Once again, this proverb has turned out to be true. Several people have contributed to the writing and publishing of this book, and I would like to thank all of them. In particular, I would like to thank Domenico Ferrari and Andres Albanese from the International Computer Science Institute (ICSI) in Berkeley, Dieter Hogrefe from the Institute for Computer Science and Applied Mathematics (IAM) of the University of Berne, and Peter Trachsel from the Swiss Federal Office of Information Technology and Systems (BFI) for giving me the opportunity and encouragement to work in this interesting and most challenging field. The book has gained a lot from discussions with and information provided by Thomas Beth (University of Karlsruhe), Daniel Bleichenbacher (ETH Zürich), Marcel Frauenknecht (BFI), Andreas Greulich (BFI), Arnold Grossmann (University of Berne), Phil Janson (IBM), Piers McMahon (ICL), Rich Salz (OSF), Basie von Solms (Rand Afrikaans University), Gene Tsudik (IBM), and Peer Wichmann (University of Karlsruhe). I'd also like to thank Artech House, Inc. for publishing the book, and Theron Shreve, Kimberly Collignon, and Judi Stone for making the publishing process most convenient to me. It has been a big pleasure to work with all of them.

Chapter 1

Introduction

The aim of this chapter is to lobby for the use of authentication and key distribution systems in networked and distributed environments. In Section 1.1 we briefly introduce the most important terms that are used in this book, and in Section 1.2 we overview the OSI security architecture. In Section 1.3 we focus on authentication and key distribution, and in Section 1.4 we summarize the notation that is used to subsequently describe the cryptographic protocols that the authentication and key distribution systems implement.

1.1 TERMINOLOGY

The field of computer science is filled with ill-defined terminology used by different authors in conflicting and sometimes even contradictory ways. We sacrifice the first section of this introductory chapter to work against this tradition, and to introduce and define the most important terms that are used in this book.

According to Webster's Encyclopedia, the term *information* refers to "knowledge communicated or received concerning a particular fact or circumstance" in general, and "data that can be coded for processing by a computer or similar device" in computer science. This definition is fairly broad and not too precise. However, it is sufficient for this book. Anybody who is interested in a more precise and formal definition of information is referred to Shannon's communication or information theory [1,2].

In accordance with the definition of information given above, we use the term information technology (IT) to refer to any kind of technology that deals with information. In particular, IT focuses on the question(s) of how to effectively store, process, and transmit data that represents and codes information. Similarly, we use the term IT security to refer to the special field of IT that deals with security-related issues. IT security comprises both computer and communication security:

- The aim of *computer security* is to preserve computing resources against abuse and unauthorized use, as well as to protect data that represents and codes information from accidental or deliberate damage, disclosure, and modification (Baker, 1991; Amoroso, 1994).

- The aim of *communication security* is to protect data that represents and codes information during its transmission in computer networks and distributed systems. We use the term *network security* as a synonym for communication security (Davies and Price, 1984; Devargas, 1993).

According to (Tanenbaum, 1988), the term *computer network* refers to an interconnected collection of autonomous computer systems. Two computer systems are interconnected if they are able to exchange data. In addition to that, the systems are autonomous if there doesn't exist a clear master/slave relationship between them. For example, a system with one control unit and several slaves is not a network; nor is a large computer with remote card readers, printers, and terminals.

There is considerable confusion in the literature about what exactly distinguishes a distributed system from a computer network. Referring to Lamport, a *distributed system* consists of a collection of distinct processes that are spatially separated and that communicate with each other by exchanging messages.[1] In addition to that, Lamport refers to a system as a distributed system if the message transmission delay is not negligible compared to the time between events in a single process [3]. Note that this definition is well suited to discuss time, clocks, and temporal ordering of events in a distributed environment.

Again referring to (Tanenbaum, 1988), the key distinction between a computer network and a distributed system is that in a distributed system, the existence of

---

[1]In a more humorous note, Lamport has also defined a distributed system as a "system that stops you from getting work done when a machine you've never seen crashes."

multiple autonomous computer systems is transparent, and not necessarily visible to the user. In principle, the user can type a command to run a program, and it runs. It is up to the operating system to select the best processor available for the program to run, to find and transport all input data to that processor, and to put the results as output data in the appropriate place. In other words, the user of a distributed system must not be aware that there are multiple processors involved, and the distributed system looks like a virtual uniprocessor. Note that in this case, a distributed system can be seen as a special case of a computer network, namely one whose software gives it a high degree of cohesiveness and transparency. Thus the distinction between a computer network and a distributed system lies within the software in general and the operating system in particular, rather than within the hardware.

In accordance with the security frameworks that are being developed by the Joint Technical Committee 1 (JTC1) of the International Organization for Standardization (ISO) and the International Electrotechnical Committee (IEC) (ISO/IEC, 1993a), we use the term *principal* to refer to a human or system entity that is registered in and authenticatable to a computer network or distributed system. Users, hosts, and processes are commonly considered as principals:

- A *user* is made accountable and ultimately responsible for his activities within a computer network or distributed system.

- A *host* is an addressable entity within a computer network or distributed system. The entity is typically addressed either by its name or by its network layer address.

- A *process* is an instantiation of a program running on a particular host. It is common to use the *client/server model* to distinguish between client and server processes:

    - A *client process* (client) is a process that requests and eventually obtains a network service, whereas

    - a *server process* (server) provides the service. In this terminology, a service refers to a coherent set of abstract functionality, and a server is typically a continuously running daemon that specializes in providing the functionality.

In general, a process can act either as client or server. For example, in a UNIX system a print server is usually created by and associated with the superuser.

On the one hand, the print server acts as a server for printing requests by clients; and on the other hand, the print server acts as a client when the server requests files to print from a file server.

The client/server model provides an attractive paradigm for designing and implementing distributed systems and corresponding applications. In the simplest case, a service is implemented by just one server. But sometimes it is more convenient to have two or more servers working simultaneously to provide a specific service. One point is that a single server may become overloaded, or may not be sufficiently close to all users in a networked or distributed environment. Another point is availability; if a service is replicated, it does not matter if some of the replicas are down or unavailable. Often, the fact that a service is replicated is transparent to the user, meaning that the user does not know whether there's a single copy of the service or there are replicas. The study and development of techniques to securely replicate services has become a new and fast growing area of research [4,5].

The ISO uses the term *standard* to refer to a documented agreement containing technical specifications or other precise criteria to be used consistently as rules, guidelines, or definitions of characteristics to ensure that materials, products, processes and services are fit for their purpose. Consequently, an *open system standard* is a standard that specifies an *open system* and allows manufacturers to build corresponding products, whereas an *open system* is a system that conforms to open system standards.

In 1978, the ISO/IEC JTC1 proposed a reference model for open systems interconnection (OSI-RM) as a preeminent model for structuring and understanding communication functions within open systems. The OSI-RM follows the widely accepted structuring technique of layering, and the communication functions are thus partitioned into a hierarchical set of layers. In particular, the OSI-RM specifies seven layers of communications system functionality, from the physical layer at the bottom to the application layer at the top. The layers are overviewed in Table 1.1. Instead of discussing every single layer of the OSI-RM, we assume that you, as reader of this book, are familiar with the model and its layers.

The OSI-RM is useful because it provides a commonly used terminology and defines a structure for data communication standards. The OSI-RM was approved as an international standard in 1982 (IS 7498). Two years later, the Telecommunication Standardization Sector of the International Telecommunication Union, namely the ITU-T[2], adopted the OSI-RM in its recommendation X.200, too.

---

[2]The ITU-T was formerly known as Consultative Committee on International Telegraphy and Telephony (CCITT).

Table 1.1
The Seven Layers of the OSI-RM

7	Application layer
6	Presentation layer
5	Session layer
4	Transport layer
3	Network layer
2	Data link layer
1	Physical layer

The use of open system standards and open systems that conform to these standards has many advantages, and we are not going to discuss them in this book. However, we want to point out that the trend towards open systems may also negatively influence security. A corresponding report from Bell Communications Research (Bellcore) has indeed shown that "intruders were assisted in their endeavors by the openness and standardization that the telecommunications industry has undergone in the last decade" [6]. Security is thus a vital concern in open systems, and the apparent contradiction between openness and security is deceptive. In fact, it has often seduced people to buy proprietary systems instead of open systems. The assumption that has led to this purchase behavior is our strong belief in "security through obscurity." We think that to hide information about the design of a system is the best way to prevent potential attackers from learning something about the system's own vulnerabilities.

In general, a *vulnerability* refers to a weakness that can be exploited to violate a system or the information that it contains, whereas a *threat* refers to a circumstance, condition, or event with the potential to either violate security or to cause harm to system resources. Computer networks and distributed systems are susceptible to a variety of threats, and these threats can be mounted either by intruders[3] or by legitimate users. As a matter of fact, legitimate users are more powerful adversaries, since they possess internal state information not usually available to intruders.

With respect to possible threats in computer networks and distributed systems, it is common to distinguish between host and communication compromises:

- A *host compromise* is the result of a subversion of an individual host within

---

[3]The term *hacker* is often used to describe computer vandals that break into computer systems. These vandals call themselves hackers, and that is how they got the name, but in my opinion, they don't deserve it. In this book, we use the terms *intruder* and *attacker* instead.

a computer network or distributed system. Various degrees of subversion are possible, ranging from the relatively benign case of corrupting process state information to the extreme case of assuming total control of the host. There are techniques available that can be used to protect a host against compromise.

- A *communication compromise* is the result of a subversion of a communication line within a computer network or distributed system. In general, there are two classes of compromising attacks to be distinguished:

  - A *passive attack* threatens the confidentiality of data that is being transmitted. The situation is shown in Figure 1.1: the data that is being transmitted from the sender (on the right side) to the receiver (on the left side) is being observed by the intruder (in the middle). With respect to the intruder's possibilities to interpret the information that the transmitted data may represent and code, passive wiretapping and traffic analysis attacks have to be distinguished:

    * In a *passive wiretapping attack*, the intruder is able to interpret the data and to extract the information accordingly, whereas
    * in a *traffic analysis attack*, the intruder is not able to do so.

Figure 1.1   A passive attack threatens the confidentiality of information in transmission.

Note that the feasibility of a passive attack primarily depends on the physical transmission media in use. Mobile communication lines are easy to tap, whereas metallic transmission media require at least some sort of physical access. Lightwave conductors can be tapped, too, but this is quite expensive. Note that the use of concentrating and multiplexing techniques, in general, makes it more difficult to passively attack a communication line. However, it is only fair to mention that a passive attacker doesn't necessarily have to tap a communication line. Today, software packages are readily available for monitoring network traffic, primarily for the purpose of network management. However, the same software packages are also effective at eavesdropping and eventually capturing passwords as they are transmitted over communication lines. One popular example is LANWatch from FTP Software.

— An *active attack* threatens the integrity and/or availability of data that are being transmitted. The situation is shown in Figure 1.2. In this case, the intruder is able to observe and control the data that is flowing by. In general, the intruder can modify, extend, delete, and replay data units. In addition to that, he or she can also flood a receiver and cause a denial of service.

Figure 1.2   An active attack threatens the integrity and/or availability of data in transmission.

Very often, passive and active attacks are used together to effectively cause a communication compromise. For example, a passive wiretapping attack can be launched to grab authentication information that is being transmitted in the clear, and this authentication information can then be used for a replay attack. Having this possibility in mind, it is obvious that password-based authentication is not sufficiently secure in networked and distributed environments, and this is what this book is all about.

1.2   OSI SECURITY ARCHITECTURE

In order to extend the field of application of the OSI-RM, the ISO/IEC JTC1 appended a security architecture in 1989 (ISO/IEC, 1989), and the ITU-T adopted the architecture in its recommendation X.800 (ITU, 1991). In fact, ISO 7498-2 and ITU-T X.800 describe the same security architecture, and in this book we use the term *OSI security architecture* to refer to both of them.

The OSI security architecture provides a general description of security services and related mechanisms, and discusses their interrelationships. It also shows how the security services map onto a network architecture, and discusses their appropriate placement within the OSI-RM. The security services and the corresponding security mechanisms are briefly overviewed in the following subsections.

Table 1.2
Classes of OSI Security Services

1	Peer entity authentication service
	Data origin authentication service
2	Access control service
3	Connection confidentiality service
	Connectionless confidentiality service
	Selected field confidentiality service
	Traffic flow confidentiality service
4	Connection integrity service with recovery
	Connection integrity service without recovery
	Selected field connection integrity service
	Connectionless integrity service
	Selected field connectionless integrity service
5	Non-repudiation with proof of origin
	Non-repudiation with proof of delivery

1.2.1   Security Services

The OSI security architecture distinguishes between five classes of security services: authentication, access control, data confidentiality, data integrity, and non-repudiation (compare Table 1.2).

1. *Authentication services* are to provide for the authentication of communicating peer entities or for the authentication of data origins.

   - A *peer entity authentication service* is to provide the ability to verify that a peer entity in an association is the one it claims to be. In particular, a peer entity authentication service provides assurance that an entity is not attempting to masquerade or perform an unauthorized replay of some previous association. Peer entity authentication is typically performed either during a connection establishment phase or, occasionally, during a data transfer phase.

- A *data origin authentication service* is to allow the sources of data received to be verified to be as claimed. A data origin authentication service, however, cannot provide protection against the duplication or modification of data units. In this case, a data integrity service must be used in conjunction with a data origin authentication service. Data origin authentication is typically provided during a data transfer phase.

Authentication services are important because they are required for authorization and accountability. Authorization refers to the process of granting rights, which includes the granting of access based on access rights. Accountability refers to the property that ensures that the actions of a principal may be traced uniquely to this principal.

2. *Access control services* are to provide for the protection of system resources against unauthorized use. Access control services are closely tied to authentication services: a user or a process acting on a user's behalf must be authenticated before an access control service can effectively mediate access to a system resource. In general, access control services are the most commonly thought of services in both computer and communication security.

3. *Data confidentiality services* are to provide for the protection of data from unauthorized disclosure.

   - A *connection confidentiality service* is to provide confidentiality of all data transmitted in a connection.

   - A *connectionless confidentiality service* is to provide confidentiality of single data units.

   - A *selective field confidentiality service* is to provide confidentiality of specific fields within the data during a connection or in a single data unit.

   - A *traffic flow confidentiality service* is to provide protection of information that may otherwise be compromised or indirectly derived from a traffic analysis.

4. *Data integrity services* are to provide for the protection of data from unauthorized modifications.

   - A *connection integrity service with recovery* is to provide integrity of data in a connection. The loss of integrity is recovered if possible.

- A *connection integrity service without recovery* is to provide integrity of data in a connection. In this case, the loss of integrity is not recovered.

- A *selected field connection integrity service* is to provide integrity of specific fields within the data during a connection.

- A *connectionless integrity service* is to provide integrity of single data units.

- A *selected field connectionless integrity service* is to provide integrity of specific fields within single data units.

Note that on a connection, the use of a peer entity authentication service at the start of the connection and a connection integrity service during the connection can jointly provide for the corroboration of the source of all data units transferred on the connection, the integrity of those data units, and may additionally provide for the detection of duplication of data units, for example by using sequence numbers.

5. *Non-repudiation services* are to provide some sort of protection against the originator of a message or action denying that he or she has originated the message or the action, as well as against the recipient of a message denying that he or she has received the message. Consequently, there are two non-repudiation services to be distinguished:

- A *non-repudiation service with proof of origin* is to provide the recipient of a message with a proof of origin, whereas

- a *non-repudiation service with proof of delivery* is to provide the sender of a message with a proof of delivery.

Non-repudiation services are becoming increasingly important in the context of electronic data interchange (EDI) and electronic commerce on the Internet.

1.2.2 Security Mechanisms

The OSI security architecture distinguishes between specific security mechanisms and pervasive security mechanisms. We are following this distinction in this subsection, too.

Specific Security Mechanisms

The OSI security architecture enumerates eight specific security mechanisms (compare Table 1.3).

Table 1.3
OSI Specific Security Mechanisms

1	Encipherment
2	Digital signature mechanisms
3	Access control mechanisms
4	Data integrity mechanisms
5	Authentication exchange mechanisms
6	Traffic padding mechanisms
7	Routing control mechanisms
8	Notarization mechanisms

1. *Encipherment* is used either to protect the confidentiality of data units and traffic flow information, or to support or complement other security mechanisms. The cryptographic techniques that are used for encipherment are overviewed in the subsequent section.

2. *Digital signature mechanisms* are used to provide an electronic analogue of handwritten signatures for electronic documents. Similar to handwritten signatures, digital signatures must not be forgeable, a recipient must be able to verify it, and the signer must not be able to repudiate it later. Again, we postpone the discussion of digital signatures to the subsequent section.

3. *Access control mechanisms* use the authenticated identities of principals, information about these principals, or capabilities to determine and enforce access rights. If a principal attempts to use an unauthorized resource, or an authorized resource with an improper type of access, the access control function rejects the attempt and may additionally report the incident for the purposes of generating an alarm and recording it as part of a security audit trail.

4. *Data integrity mechanisms* are used to protect the integrity of either single data units and fields within these data units or sequences of data units and fields within these sequences of data units. Note that data integrity mechanisms, in general, don't protect against replay attacks. Protecting the integrity

of a sequence of data units and fields within these data units generally requires some form of explicit ordering, such as sequence numbering, time stamping, or cryptographic chaining.

5. *Authentication exchange mechanisms* are used to verify the claimed identities of principals. In accordance with ITU-T X.509 (ITU, 1987), an authentication exchange mechanism is strong if it relies on the use of cryptographic techniques to protect the messages that are exchanged. Strong authentication exchange mechanisms are at the core of this book and not further elaborated at this point.

6. *Traffic padding mechanisms* are used to protect against traffic analysis attacks. Traffic padding refers to the generation of spurious instances of communication, spurious data units, and spurious data within data units. The aim is not to reveal if data that is being transmitted actually represents and codes information. Consequently, traffic padding mechanisms can only be effective if they are protected by a data confidentiality service.

7. *Routing control mechanisms* can be used to either dynamically or by pre-arrangement choose specific routes for data transmission. Communicating systems may, on detection of persistent passive or active attacks, wish to instruct the network service provider to establish a connection via a different route. Similarly, data carrying certain security labels may be forbidden by a security policy to pass through certain networks, relays, or links.

8. *Notarization mechanisms* can be used to assure certain properties of the data communicated between two or more entities, such as its integrity, origin, time, or destination. The assurance is provided by a trusted third party in a testifiable manner.

Pervasive Security Mechanisms

Pervasive security mechanisms are not specific to any particular service, and some of these mechanisms can be regarded as aspects of security management, too. The importance of pervasive security mechanisms, in general, is directly related to the level of security required. The OSI security architecture enumerates five pervasive security mechanisms (compare Table 1.4).

Table 1.4
OSI Pervasive Security Mechanisms

1	Trusted functionality
2	Security labels
3	Event detection
4	Security audit trail
5	Security recovery

1. The general concept of *trusted functionality* can be used either to extend the scope or to establish the effectiveness of other security mechanisms. Any functionality that directly provides, or provides access to security mechanisms, should be trustworthy.

2. System resources may have *security labels* associated with them (e.g., to indicate sensitivity levels). It is often necessary to convey the appropriate security label with data in transit. A security label may be additional data associated with the data transferred or may be implicit (e.g., implied by the use of a specific key to encipher data or implied by the context of the data such as the source or route).

3. Security-relevant *event detection* can be used to detect apparent violations of security.

4. A security audit refers to an independent review and examination of system records and activities in order to test for adequacy of system controls, to ensure compliance with established policy and operational procedures, to detect breaches in security, and to recommend any indicated changes in control, policy, and procedures. Consequently, a *security audit trail* refers to data collected and potentially used to facilitate a security audit.

5. *Security recovery* deals with requests from mechanisms such as event handling and management functions, and takes recovery actions as the result of applying a set of rules.

Remember that the OSI security architecture hasn't been developed to solve a particular network security problem, but to provide the network security community with a terminology that can be commonly used to describe and discuss security-related problems and corresponding solutions. We are going to use the terminology to further describe and discuss authentication and key distribution in computer networks and distributed systems, too.

1.3 AUTHENTICATION AND KEY DISTRIBUTION

We have already mentioned in the preface that you, as a reader of this book, are assumed to be familiar with cryptology and the use of cryptographic protocols in networked and distributed environments. If you truly fulfill this assumption, you should skip this section and go to Chapter 2. If you don't fulfill this assumption, you should put this book away, read one of the books cited in the preface, and continue reading this book afterward (if you still feel like doing so). However, we assume that most readers know a little about cryptology, without knowing whether they actually know enough to understand the rest of this book. This section is intended to give those readers a survey on topics they should be familiar with or can become familiar with. We first overview some cryptographic techniques, and focus then on the use of these techniques in authentication and key distribution systems.

1.3.1 Cryptographic Techniques

In general, *cryptology* refers to the science of secure communications.[4] Cryptology comprises both cryptography and cryptanalysis. Let's have a brief look at one-way hash functions, secret key cryptography, and public key cryptography.

One-Way Hash Functions

One-way functions are of central importance in cryptology. Informally speaking, a one-way function is easy to compute, but hard to invert. More formally speaking, a function $f : A \longrightarrow B$ is a *one-way function* if $f(x)$ is easy to compute for all $x \in A$, but it is computationally infeasible when given $y \in f(A) = B$ to find an $x \in A$ such that $f(x) = y$. This definition is not precise in a mathematical sense, because it doesn't resolve what is "easy" and what is "computationally infeasible." It is important to note that the existence of one-way functions is still an unproven assumption and that, until today, no function has shown to be one-way. Obviously, a sufficiently large domain prohibiting an exhaustive search is a necessary but not sufficient condition for a function to be one-way.

---

[4]The word "cryptology" is derived from the Greek words "kryptós" for "hidden" and lógos for "word." Consequently, cryptology can be translated as "the science of hidden words."

It is not required, in general, that a one-way function be invertible, and distinct input values may be mapped to the same output value. As a matter of fact, a one-way function $f : A \longrightarrow B$ for which $\mid B \mid \ll \mid A \mid$ is also called a *one-way hash function*. If, in addition to these conditions for one-way hash functions, it is also computationally infeasible to find distinct $x_1, x_2 \in A$ such that $f(x_1) = f(x_2)$, then f is a *collision-resistant* one-way hash function. Examples of collision-resistant one-way hash functions are MD4 (Rivest, 1992), MD5 (Rivest and Dusse, 1992), and the *secure hash standard* (SHS) proposed by the U.S. National Institute of Standards and Technology (NIST) in Federal Information Processing Standard (FIPS) 180 (NIST, 1993).

Secret Key Cryptography

In *secret key cryptography*, a secret key is established and shared between communicating parties, and this key is used to subsequently encrypt and decrypt messages. Therefore, secret key cryptography is also called *symmetric cryptography*.

Secret key cryptography has been in use for thousands of years in a variety of forms. Modern implementations usually take the form of algorithms, which are executed by computer systems in hardware, firmware, or even software. The majority of secret key cryptosystems are based on operations that can be performed very efficiently by computer systems. In theory, to design a secure secret key cryptosystem seems to be possible without having a deep background in mathematics and cryptology. By combining a set of more or less complex transformations, such as permutations and transpositions, one can create a system that appears to be too difficult to analyze even for a powerful enemy. In spite of the fact that the history of cryptographical failures is long and rich, most of these failures were either due to the fact that the number and complexity of the transformations was severely limited in the precomputer age, or that too much structure was introduced for the sake of analyzability, which in turn allowed an enemy to successfully perform a cryptanalysis.

Examples of secret key cryptosystems that are in widespread use today are the *data encryption standard* (DES) (NIST, 1977), *triple DES*, the *international data encryption algorithm* (IDEA) (Lai, 1992), as well as *RC2*, *RC4*, and *RC5* (Rivest, 1995). The *fast encryption algorithm* (FEAL) should no longer be used, as it has shown to be vulnerable to differential cryptanalysis.

Public Key Cryptography

The idea of having one-way functions with trapdoors has led to the invention of *public key cryptography* (Diffie and Hellman, 1976). From a practical point of view, a public key cryptosystem is a cryptosystem in which a user has a pair of mathematically related keys. The pair consists of a public key that can be published without doing any harm to the system's security, and a private key that is assumed to never leave the possession of its owner [7]. For both the public and the private key it is computationally infeasible to derive one from the other. Today, the most widely deployed public key cryptosystem is RSA, invented by Rivest, Shamir and Adleman at the Massachusetts Institute of Technology (MIT) (Rivest, Shamir, and Adleman, 1978).

The application of public key cryptography requires an authentication framework that binds users' public keys and users' identities. A public key certificate is a certified proof of such binding vouched for by a trusted third-party, called a *certification authority* (CA). The use of a CA alleviates the responsibility of individual users to verify directly the correctness of other users' public keys.

Public key cryptography can in theory be more convenient than secret key cryptography since it is not necessary for two parties wishing to authenticate each other to share a secret key. Hence, a less complicated key distribution system may be required. Also, public key cryptography makes it possible to place the authentication information under the direct control of the system user. For access control, this is especially helpful since secret authentication information need not be distributed throughout the system.

However, public key systems generally require arithmetic operations that are difficult for small microprocessors. This can cause problems in the design of authentication systems since it is often necessary for the cryptographic algorithms to be implemented on a small device with limited processing power. It can be very difficult to obtain satisfactory performance from a smart card or reader/writer in terms of public key operations. This deficiency can be compensated for to some extent by distributing operations between the authentication system and the host computer system. In addition to that, advances in integrated circuit technology are increasing the capabilities of devices such as smart cards to the point where an acceptable level of performance can be attained in the implementation of public key algorithms. Hybrid approaches are also possible, where public key cryptography is used to distribute keys for use by secret key cryptosystem.

It has already been mentioned that digital signatures are to provide an electronic analogue of handwritten signatures for electronic documents and that, similar to handwritten signatures, digital signatures must not be forgeable; recipients must be able to verify them, and the signers must not be able to repudiate them later. However, a major difference between a handwritten and a digital signature is due to the fact that the digital signature can't be constant, and must be a function of the document that it signs. If this were not the case, then a signature, due to its electronic nature, could be cut and pasted to any document at will. In addition to that, a digital signature must be a function of the entire document that it signs. Again, if this were not the case, a signed document could be altered at will.

Arbitrated digital signature schemes are based on secret key cryptography. In principle, a trusted third party validates the signature and forwards it on the signer's behalf. True digital signature schemes come along without trusted third parties taking an active role. They require the use of public key cryptography: Signed messages are sent directly from signers to recipients. In general, a *digital signature scheme* consists of

- A key generation algorithm that randomly selects a public key pair;

- A signature algorithm that takes as input a message and a private key, and that generates as output a digital signature for the message; and

- A signature verification algorithm that takes as input a digital signature and a public key, and that generates as output an information bit according to whether the signature is consistent with some valid message for the private key corresponding to the given public key.

The bandwidth limitation of public key cryptography is unimportant, due to the use of one-way hash functions as auxiliaries. Examples of public key-based digital signature schemes are RSA, ElGamal (ElGamal, 1984; ElGamal, 1985), and the *digital signature standard* (DSS) proposed by the U.S. National Institute of Standards and Technology (NIST) in Federal Information Processing Standard (FIPS) 186 (NIST, 1994).

1.3.2 Authentication

In general, *authentication* refers to the process of verifying the claimed identity of a principal. Authentication results in authenticity, meaning that the verifying principal (*verifier*) can be sure that the verified principal (*claimant*) is the one he or she claims to be.

It is common to divide the techniques that are used for authentication into three categories, depending on whether a technique is based on

- Something the claimer knows (proof by knowledge);

- Something the claimer possesses (proof by possession);

- Some biometric characteristics of the claimer (proof by property).

Examples for the first category are *personal identification numbers* (PINs), passwords, and *transaction authentication numbers* (TANs), whereas examples for the second category are keys, identification cards, and other physical devices or personal tokens. Historically the first biometric characteristics that were used for authentication were fingerprints. Today, it is possible to use other characteristics, too. Examples are facial images, retinal images, and voice patterns. However, in computer networks and distributed systems, most of the authentication mechanisms in use today are based on proof by knowledge.

Password-Based Authentication

In most computer networks and distributed systems, protection of resources is achieved by direct login to each host accessed using passwords, with users selecting the password and transmitting it in the clear and unprotected. This password-based authentication has several drawbacks, and we are going to mention only a few of them:

- Users tend to select passwords that are not randomly distributed. This problem is well known and not necessarily related to computer networks and distributed systems [8,9].

- It is not convenient for a user who has several accounts on different hosts to have to remember a password for each of them, as well as to enter it each time he or she changes the host. Instead, the user should be known as a single user to the computer network or distributed system as a whole.

- The transmission of a password itself is exposed to passive eavesdropping and subsequent replay attacks.

Mainly because of the last drawback, password-based authentication is not suitable for use in computer networks and distributed systems. Passwords sent across networks are too easy to intercept and use to impersonate users. While this vulnerability has been long known, it was recently demonstrated on a major scale with the discovery of planted password collecting routines at critical points within the Internet.[5]

There are situations in which it is really annoying that the designers opted for password-based authentication. For example, in the United States cellular phones transmit the telephone number of the phone and a password when making a call. If the password corresponds to the telephone number, the telephone company accepts the call and bills the account that corresponds to the telephone number. The problem is obvious: an attacker can eavesdrop on cellular phone transmissions and clone a phone, meaning he can make a phone that uses the same telephone number and password pair. Indeed, this is a problem, and criminals clone phones either to steal phone service or to make untraceable calls.

Address-Based Authentication

One way to overcome the problems of password-based authentication is address-based authentication, as for example incorporated in the Berkeley r-tools (`rlogin`, `rsh`, and `rcp`) for UNIX, or the proxy database for VMS. Address-based authentication does not rely on sending passwords around the network, but rather assumes that the identity of the source can be inferred based on the network address from which packets arrive. The basic idea is that each host stores information that specifies accounts on other hosts that should have access to its resources. In UNIX, each host may have a file named `/etc/hosts.equiv` containing a list of trusted hostnames. Users with the same username on both the local and remote host may use the Berkeley r-tools from a trusted host without having to supply a password. Individual users may set up a similar private equivalence list with the `.rhosts` file in their home directories. Each line in this file contains a hostname and a username separated by a space. An entry in a user's remote `.rhosts` file permits the user who is logged into the system specified by hostname to log into the remote system without supplying a password.

Note that the idea of trusted hosts is no general solution to the authentication problem in computer networks and distributed systems. As a matter of fact, trusted hosts can even pose a serious security threat. The point is that host authentication mechanisms can always be defeated, and if an attacker is able to break into an account in a host that is trusted by other hosts, the user's account on the other hosts are compromised, too. The use of `.rhosts` files poses an additional security threat because the system administrator is, in general, unable to exclusively control

---

[5]Compare CERT Advisory CA-94:01, "Ongoing network monitoring attacks," February 3, 1994.

access to the system via the r-tools. Users are likely to tailor their .rhosts files more for convenience than for security.

Depending on the environment, address-based authentication may be more or less secure than sending passwords in the clear. In either case, it is more convenient, and it is therefore the authentication mechanism of choice in most computer networks and distributed systems today.

Cryptographic Authentication

The basic idea of a cryptographic authentication is that a claimant A proves his or her identity to a verifier B by performing a cryptographic operation of a quantity that either both know or B supplies. The cryptographic operation performed by A is based on a cryptographic key. This cryptographic key can either be a secret key or a private key from a public key cryptosystem.

In general, cryptographic authentication can be made more secure than either password-based or address-based authentication. In addition to that, new techniques based on zero-knowledge proofs may provide even more powerful authentication mechanisms [10,11]. These techniques demand rather intensive mathematical computations, but they present several attractive features for authentication. First, they allow the claimer to prove that he or she knows the right identification secret without actually transferring any knowledge about that secret to the verifier. Second, some of the zero-knowledge schemes that have been proposed so far are such that verification of the authentication messages of any claimer all require the same public information, which avoids altogether the problem of key distribution exhibited by DES- or RSA-based authentication mechanisms.

Despite the apparent simplicity of the basic design principles for authentication protocols, designing realistic protocols is notoriously difficult and several published protocols have exhibited substantial or subtle security problems. During the last decade, research efforts have focused on providing tools needed for developing authentication and key distribution protocols with some formal assurance of security. Most notably, formal tools for testing protocols were developed; for example, the BAN logic [12] and its successor, the GNY logic [13]. Instead of devising specific protocols, these methodologies provide a means for showing that appropriate beliefs are attained as a result of running an authentication protocol.

1.3.3 Key Distribution

Most of the security services that are enumerated in the OSI security architecture are based on cryptographic mechanisms, and the use of these mechanisms, in general, requires a corresponding key management. According to the ISO, *key management* has to deal with "the generation, storage, distribution, deletion, archiving and application of keys in accordance with a security policy" (ISO/IEC, 1989). Key management is carried out with protocols, and many of the important properties of key management protocols do not depend on the underlying cryptographic algorithms, but rather on the structure of the messages exchanged. Therefore, security leaks and vulnerabilities do not come from weak cryptographic algorithms, but rather from mistakes in higher levels of the protocol design.

The working group (WG) 802.10 of the Institute of Electrical and Electronic Engineers (IEEE) was formed in May of 1988 to address the security needs of local and metropolitan area networks. The WG is cosponsored by the IEEE Technical Committee on Computer Communications and by the IEEE Technical Committee on Security and Privacy. Within IEEE 802.10, work on cryptographic key management began in May of 1989. The key management model and protocol that is being standardized by IEEE 802.10 supports three classes of key distribution techniques, namely manual key distribution, center-based key distribution, and certificate-based key distribution (IEEE, 1995). We are going to use this classification in this book, too.

Manual Key Distribution

Manual key distribution techniques use offline delivery methods to establish pairwise or multicast cryptographic keys. Manual key distribution techniques, in general, may be cumbersome and have scalability problems. Also, they do not provide any authentication other than that provided by the corresponding offline delivery method. Therefore, the strength of the procedures used for offline delivery of the cryptographic keys is extremely important.

In many cases, however, manual delivery of cryptographic keys is required only once per user, and distribution of additional keying material can be performed using the manually distributed key as a *key encryption key* (KEK). The encrypted keying material can then be distributed using any convenient method. Manual key distribution is suitable for multicast key distribution. In fact, it is often the most efficient way to distribute group keys, especially to large groups.

Center-Based Key Distribution

Center-based key distribution techniques may be used to establish pairwise or multicast cryptographic keys between the communicating parties via a trusted third party. This trusted third party can either be

- A *key distribution center* (KDC);

- A *key translation center* (KTC).

Center-based key distribution covers both KDCs and KTCs. The corresponding key distribution protocols depend upon the manual distribution of KEKs to provide confidentiality and integrity protection of for the distributed keys.

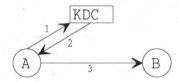

Figure 1.3   The pull model for center-based key distribution.

Most existing key distribution methods have been tailored to specific scenarios and applications. For example, any scheme relying on timestamps favors the local environment, where all users have access to a commonly trusted time server. While requiring tightly synchronized clocks in the wide area is conceivable, it is certainly harder. More importantly, existing schemes make specific assumptions about network configuration and connectivity models. For instance, they may dictate a specific communication paradigm for contacting a trusted server or KDC: When a principal A needs a key to communicate with another principal B, Kerberos for example requires that A obtains the desired key from the KDC prior to communicating with B. This paradigm is sometimes also referred to as the *pull model* (compare Figure 1.3).

By contrast, in the same situation, the U.S. standard for financial institution key management (ANSI X9.17) specifies that A must contact B first, and let B get the necessary key from the KDC (ANSI, 1985). This paradigm is sometimes also referred to as the *push model* (compare Figure 1.4). A pushes B to contact the KDC and request a session key accordingly.

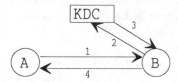

Figure 1.4   The push model for center-based key distribution.

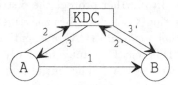

Figure 1.5   The mixed model for center-based key distribution.

It is important to note, however, that neither the push model nor the pull model is better than the other, and that both models are justified in their respective environments. In a local area environment, for which Kerberos was originally designed, requiring clients to obtain the keys makes a lot of sense because it distributes the burden over many clients, thus alleviating the task of the few shared servers. In a wide area environment, for which X9.17 was designed, the opposite approach is justified because there are typically many more clients than servers, and KDCs are typically located closer to servers than clients. Under such circumstances, the amount of system definition in terms of configuration, and the costs of the connections between clients and the KDCs required by the Kerberos approach may become prohibitive in a wide area environment. It is even possible to combine the two approaches and to come up with a mixed model for center-based key distribution (compare Figure 1.5).

Certificate-Based Key Distribution

Certificate-based key distribution techniques may be used to establish pairwise cryptographic keys. There are two classes of certificate-based key distribution techniques to be distinguished:

- A public key cryptosystem is used to encrypt a locally generated cryptographic key to protect it while it is being transfered to a remote key management entity. This is called a *key transfer*.

- A cryptographic key is cooperatively generated at both the local and remote key management entity. This is called a *key exchange* or a *key agreement*.

In general, certificate-based key distribution techniques may not be directly used to establish multicast keys. However, once pairwise cryptographic keys are established, they can be used to further protect the distribution of multicast keys.

The ITU-T recommendation X.509 describes a certificate-based key distribution scheme, where a *certification authority* (CA) authenticates registered principals' public keys (ITU, 1987). Different CAs may mutually certify their public keys, resulting in a connected graph of CAs. The initial point of trust for a particular user is the CA that registered him. For reasons of simplicity, this graph is often looked upon as a tree with optional additional connections. This tree corresponds to the *directory information tree* (DIT) of the X.500 recommendation series.

If two principals A and B both have certificates from the same CA Z, B can obtain A's public key by first obtaining A's certificate from any source and then checking the certificate with the public key of Z. If A and B are certified by different CAs X and Y, B has to construct a certification path. In essence, this is a sequence of certificates starting with a certificate issued by Y and ending with X's certificate for A, where each certificate in the path contains the public key to check the following certificate.

Certificate revocation refers to the announcement that a private key has or may have fallen into the wrong hands and that the certificate that belongs to the corresponding public key should no longer be used for authentication. In general, there are three methods for certificate revocation:

1. The first method for revocation is using timeouts and renewals of certificates. Part of the signed message that is a certificate may be a time after which the certificate should not be believed anymore. Periodically, a CA would renew certificates by signing one with a later timeout. If a key were compromised, a new key would be generated and a new certificate signed. The old certificate would only be valid until its timeout. Timeouts are not perfect revocation mechanisms because they provide only slow revocation and depend on servers having an accurate source of time. Someone who can trick a server into turning back its clock can still use expired certificates.

2. The second method for revocation is by listing all nonrevoked certificates in a directory service and believing only certificates found there. The advantage of this method is that it is almost immediate. The disadvantages are that the availability of authentication is only as good as the availability of the directory service, and that the security of revocation is only as good as the security of the directory service.

3. The third method for revocation is for CAs to periodically issue certificate revocation lists (CRLs), which list certificates that should no longer be accepted.

1.4 NOTATION

The following notation is used in this book:

- Capital letters, such as A, B, C, ..., are used to refer to principals, whereas the same letters put in italics are used to refer to the corresponding principal identifiers. Note that many publications on cryptology and cryptographic protocols use names, such as Alice and Bob, to refer to principals. This is a convenient way of making things unambiguous with relatively few words, since the pronoun "she" can be used for Alice, and "he" can be used for Bob. However, the advantages and disadvantages of this naming scheme are controversial, and we are not going to use it in this book.

- K is used to refer to a secret key, which is basically a key of a secret key cryptosystem.

- The pair (k, k^{-1}) is used to refer to a public key pair, whereas k is used to refer to the public key and k^{-1} is used to refer to the corresponding private key.

In either case, key subscripts may be used to indicate principals. In general, capital letter subscripts are used for long-term keys, and small letter subscripts are used for short-term keys. For example, K_A is used to refer to A's long-term secret key, whereas k_b is used to refer to B's short-term public key.

- The term $\{m\}K$ is used to refer to a message m that is encrypted with the secret key K. The same key K is used for decryption, so $\{\{m\}K\}K$ equals m. If K is used to compute and verify a *message authentication code* (MAC) for message m, then the term $\langle m \rangle K$ is used to refer to $\{h(m)\}K$, with h being collision-resistant one-way hash function.

- Similarly, the term $\{m\}k$ is used to refer to a message m that is encrypted with the public key k. The message can only be decrypted with the corresponding private key k^{-1}. If a public key cryptosystem is used to digitally sign messages, the private key is used for signing and the corresponding public key is used for verifying signatures. In this case, the term $\{m\}k^{-1}$ is used to refer to a digital signature giving message recovery, and $\langle m \rangle k^{-1}$ is used to refer to a digital signature with appendix (ISO/IEC, 1989). Note that in the second case, $\langle m \rangle k^{-1}$ in fact abbreviates $m, \{h(m)\}k^{-1}$, with h being again a collision-resistant one-way hash function.

- In accordance with international standardization, $X \ll Y \gg$ is used to refer to a certificate that has been issued by X for Y's public key. Note that $X \ll Y \gg$, in principle, implies that X has certified the binding of Y's long-term public key k_Y with Y's identity. For example, an ITU-T X.509-certificate of CA Z for principal A is referred to as $Z \ll A \gg$ and consists of the following information digitally signed by Z:

$$Z \ll A \gg = \langle SN, AI, Z, A, k_A, L \rangle k_Z^{-1}$$

  In this expression, SN is the serial number of the certificate, AI is an identifier of the algorithm that was used to digitally sign the certificate, Z and A are the names of the CA and principal A, respectively, k_A is A's public key, and L is the lifetime of the certificate.

- T is used to refer to a *timestamp*. Timestamp subscripts may be used to imply a temporal ordering.

- N is used to refer to a *nonce*. In short, a nonce is a quantity that any given user of a cryptographic protocol is supposed to use only once. Various forms of nonce are a timestamp, a sequence number, or a large and unpredictable random number. In our notation, we use small letters in nonce subscripts to indicate particular principals. Small letters are used mainly because of the short-term nature of nonces.

In general, a protocol specifies the format and relative timing of information exchanged between communicating parties. In the protocol descriptions that follow, the term

$i: \mathrm{P} \longrightarrow \mathrm{Q} : m$

is used to refer to step i, in which P is assumed to transmit a message m to Q. Note that the notation of $\longrightarrow$ must be interpreted with care. The messages are sent in environments, where error, corruption, loss, and delay may occur. There is nothing in the environment to guarantee that messages are really made in numerical order by the principals indicated, received in numerical order or at all by the principals indicated, or received solely by the principals indicated [14,15].

REFERENCES

[1] C.E. Shannon, "A Mathematical Theory of Communication," *The Bell System Technical Journal*, Vol. 27, July/October 1948, pp. 379 – 423/623 – 656.

[2] C.E. Shannon, "Communication Theory of Secrecy Systems," *The Bell System Technical Journal*, Vol. 28, October 1949, pp. 656 – 715.

[3] L. Lamport, "Time, Clocks, and the Ordering of Events in a Distributed System," *Communications of the ACM*, Vol. 21, July 1978, pp. 558 – 565.

[4] L. Gong, "Increasing Availability and Security of an Authentication Service," *IEEE Journal on Selected Areas in Communications*, Vol. 11, June 1993, pp. 657 – 662.

[5] M.K. Reiter, and K.P. Birman, "How to Securely Replicate Services," *ACM Transactions on Programming Languages and Systems*, Vol. 16, 1994, pp. 986 – 1009.

[6] H.M. Kluepfel, "A Systems Engineering Approach to Security Baselines for SS7," Technical Report TM-STS-020882, Bellcore, Murray Hill, NJ, 1992.

[7] W. Diffie, "The First Ten Years of Public-Key Cryptography," *Proceedings of the IEEE*, Vol. 76, 1988, pp. 560 – 577.

[8] D.C. Feldmeier, and P.R. Karn, "UNIX Password Security — Ten Years Later," in G. Brassard, editor, *Advances in Cryptology — CRYPTO '89*, Springer-Verlag, Berlin, 1990, pp. 44 – 63.

[9] D.V. Klein, ""Foiling the Cracker": A Survey of, and Improvements to, Password Security," *in Proceedings of the USENIX UNIX Security II Symposium*, USENIX Association, Berkeley, CA, August 1990, pp. 5 – 14.

[10] A. Fiat, and A. Shamir, "How to Prove Yourself: Practical Solutions to Indetification and Signature Problems," in A.M. Odlyzko, editor, *Advances in Cryptology — CRYPTO '86*, Springer-Verlag, Berlin, 1987, pp. 186 – 194.

[11] J.J. Quisquater, and L. Guillou, "How to Explain Zero-Knowledge Protocols to Your Children," in G. Brassard, editor, *Advances in Cryptology — CRYPTO '89*, Springer-Verlag, Berlin, 1990, pp. 628 – 631.

[12] M. Burrows, M. Abadi, and R. Needham, "A Logic of Authentication," *ACM Operating Systems Review*, Vol. 23, 1989, pp. 1 – 13.

[13] L. Gong, R. Needham, and R. Yahalom, "GNY Logic Fill In," *in Proceedings of the IEEE Symposium on Security and Privacy*, IEEE Computer Society Press, Los Alamitos, CA, 1990, pp. 234 – 248.

[14] M. Abadi, and R.M. Needham, "Prudent Engineering Practice for Cryptographic Protocols," *in Proceedings of the IEEE Symposium on Security and Privacy*, IEEE Computer Society Press, Los Alamitos, CA, 1994, pp. 122 – 136.

[15] M. Abadi, and R. Needham, "Prident Engineering Practice for Cryptographic Protocols," SRC Research Report 125 No. AA-LA40B-TE, DEC Systems Research Center, Palo Alto, CA, June 1994.

Chapter 2

Kerberos

In this chapter we focus on the authentication and key distribution system Kerberos. In Section 2.1 we summarize the development of the system, and in Section 2.2 we overview its architecture. In Section 2.3 we describe the cryptographic protocols that Kerberos implements, and in Section 2.4 we discuss some extensions and new applications.

2.1 DEVELOPMENT

The authentication and key distribution system *Kerberos*[1] [1,2,3] was developed at the Massachusetts Institute of Technology (MIT) to protect the emerging network services provided by the Athena project [4,5]. The aim of Kerberos was to extend the notion of authentication, authorization, and accounting to the MIT computing and networking environment. According to the Project Athena's technical plan [6], this environment basically consists of

- Public and private workstations.

---

[1]In Greek mythology, *Kerberos* is the name of the three-headed watch dog of Hades, whose duty it was to guard the entrance of the underworld.

- Public workstations are located in areas with no or only minimal physical security;
- Private workstations are under physical and administrative control of individuals with generally no responsibility to a central network administration.

- A campus network, composed of local area networks (LANs) of varying types connected to a backbone network. The LANs are spatially dispersed and vulnerable to various attacks, whereas the backbone network devices are locked in closets and assumed to operate under moderate physical security.

- Centrally operated servers. Most of these servers are placed in locked rooms and are assumed to operate under moderate physical security with software that does not include malicious code. Only a few servers operate under considerable physical security, and these servers can be used as security servers.

Note that this environment is neither appropriate to store, process, or transmit sensitive data, such as financial records or classified data, nor to perform high-risk operations, such as controlling dangerous experiments. The risks that are considered are primarily uncontrolled use of resources by unauthorized parties, violations of the integrity of the system resources, as well as wholesale violations of privacy such as casual browsing through personal files.

In this environment, the primary security threats result from the potential of a workstation user to forge the identity of another user in order to gain unauthorized access to system resources. A workstation, including its operating system and network interface(s), is under the complete control of the user, who can attempt to masquerade as another user or host. Privacy of data being transmitted across the network is of low priority, except where it is necessary to prevent subsequent violations of security. Traffic analysis and covert channels are not addressed by Kerberos either.

The first three versions of Kerberos were used at MIT only. They are no longer in use today, and hence are not adequately covered in this book. The first version that was made publicly available was Kerberos version 4 (V4), and this version has also achieved widespread use beyond MIT. With patch level 10, officially released in December 1992, MIT Kerberos V4 is in its final state today. As a matter of fact, MIT does not anticipate ever making a new Kerberos V4 release.

Some sites require functionality that Kerberos V4 does not provide, while others have a computing and networking environment or administrative procedures that differ from MIT. As a result, work on Kerberos version 5 (V5) commenced in 1989, also fueled by discussions with Kerberos V4 users and administrators about their experience with the Kerberos model in general, and the MIT reference implementation in particular.

In September 1993, Kerberos V5 was specified as an Internet standards track protocol in RFC 1510 [7]. Again, the MIT provided a Kerberos V5 reference implementation, and the latest version of this implementation is beta version 5, officially released on May 5, 1995. This release contains numerous bug fixes, a new build system based on `autoconf` instead of `imake`, ASN.1 parsers so that ISODE (ISO development environment) is no longer required, and some further improvements and enhancements. MIT has developed and tested the Kerberos V5 reference implementation on Ultrix, SunOS, Solaris, and Linux, and others have ported it to other platforms, too.

It should be noted that Kerberos V4 and V5, although conceptually similar, are substantially different from one another, and are even competing for dominance in the marketplace. In short, Kerberos V4 has a greater installed base, is simpler, and has better performance than V5, but works only with IP addresses, whereas Kerberos V5 has a smaller installed base, is less simple and thus less efficient, but provides more functionality than V4. We will discuss the main differences between Kerberos V4 and V5 later in this chapter.

In spite of the fact that the source code of Kerberos V4 and V5 is freely available from MIT, the institute does not officially support these software releases. However, several companies have taken the reference implementations from MIT and provide commercially available and supported implementations of Kerberos, too. Information on the free releases and the commercial versions of Kerberos can be obtained by reading the Kerberos FAQ that are periodically posted to the USENET newsgroup `comp.protocols.kerberos`, or by sending e-mail to `info-kerberos@mit.edu`.

2.2 ARCHITECTURAL OVERVIEW

In the Kerberos terminology, an administration domain is called a *realm*. It is assumed that every company or organization that wishes to run Kerberos establishes a realm that is uniquely identified by a *realm name*. In theory, a Kerberos realm can support well over 100,000 users, and referring to [8], the realm `ATHENA.MIT.EDU` currently supports 25,000 users, of which about 7,000 typically log in every day.

Kerberos is based on the client/server model. Users, clients, and instantiated network services on particular hosts are typically considered as principals. Each principal is uniquely identified by a *principal identifier*. In Kerberos V4, a principal identifier has three component fields, each of which is a null-terminated case-sensitive text string of up to 40 characters. The three component fields are

- A principal name, NAME;

- An instance name, INSTANCE;

- A realm name, REALM.

Kerberos does not particularly care how the NAME and INSTANCE component fields are used. They are merely text strings. However, in practice, services have a name, and it is common to use the INSTANCE field to indicate the particular host on which the service is provided. For example, the rlogin service on the host asterix may be distinguished from the rlogin service on the host obelix. The INSTANCE field is not as useful for human users, and usually the null string is used for the instance name of a corresponding principal identifier. But as long as there is that component field in a principal identifier, the convention for human users is that it is used to denote something about the role of the user for that particular login session. For example, a user can have the principal name rolf and the instance name systemmanager or gameplayer. Presumably, rolf.systemmanager would have access to more network resources than rolf.gameplayer.

In effect, a name is just a concatenation of the principal and instance names. Kerberos could certainly have done without the concept of an instance name, and by convention principals could just use different names in their various roles. As a matter of fact, if the period were a legal character in the text string for a name[2], the names could be identical to what they currently are, without having to separate them into two component fields. With regard to the realm name, it is common to use the Internet domain name of a company or organization. Because Kerberos is case sensitive whereas the Internet domain names are case insensitive, by convention realm names are always set in uppercase.

The aim of Kerberos is to allow a client running on behalf of a particular user to prove its identity to a service or a corresponding application server without having to send data across the network that might allow an attacker to subsequently impersonate the user. In order to achieve this goal, the Kerberos model requires the existence of a trusted third party that serves as a key distribution center (KDC) in a Kerberos realm. The KDC consists of two components, namely

1. An *authentication server* (AS);

2. A set of *ticket granting servers* (TGSs).

Note that the AS and the TGSs are only logically separated components that may be processes running on the same host(s). Also note that the host(s) that

---

[2]To include a period as part of a principal or instance name, it must be quoted with a backslash.

provide these services must be carefully protected and physically secure. If an intruder is able to subvert either the AS or any of the TGSs, they can compromise the system at will.

The KDC maintains a database that includes an entry for every single principal registered in the realm. In order to allow security of the data to be the primary consideration when making operational tradeoffs about the management of Kerberos, the information that Kerberos stores is the minimum required to accomplish and manage authentication. Thus, although a Kerberos database entry is a kind of per-user record, it does not contain information such as phone numbers or office addresses, which are not used for authentication. As a matter of fact, the information that a Kerberos KDC stores for each principal P basically includes

- P's principal identifier;
- P's master key K_p (or P's password if P is a user);
- An expiration date for P's identity;
- The date the record was last modified;
- The identity of the principal who last modified the record;
- The maximum lifetime of tickets to be given to the principal;
- Some attributes;
- Some implementation-related data that are not visible externally, such as a key version, a master key version, or pointers to old values of the record.

One piece of information in every record, namely the master key K_p, must be kept secret. Kerberos therefore encrypts all principal master keys with a KDC master key. This encryption allows a system manager to remove copies of the KDC database from the master server, and send copies thereof to slave servers without going to extraordinary lengths to protect the privacy of these copies. Slave servers are required in large realms to provide a highly available Kerberos security service. Note that Kerberos does not store the KDC master key in the same database, but manages that key separately.

Kerberos provides several tools for the management of the KDC database. In a small realm, a set of manual tools can be used from the system administrator's console. To be used in larger realms, an automated service management system (SMS) is supported, too. In either case, the Kerberos management functions are accomplished remotely via the network, using Kerberos to authenticate any connection to the KDC database. Updates are done by a protocol that runs between an authenticated client on a workstation and the KDC database. There are update routines for adding and deactivating principal entries as well as to support user- or manager-initiated password changes. If the KDC database is not accessible, updates are temporarily disallowed.

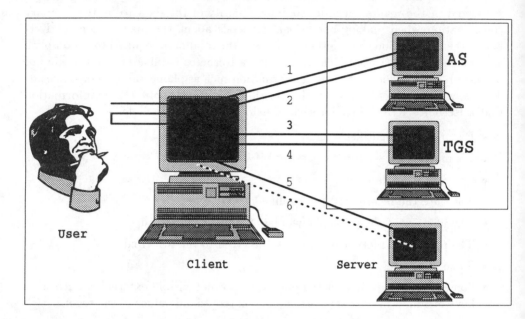

Figure 2.1   The basic Kerberos model and the corresponding protocol steps.

Figure 2.1 illustrates the basic Kerberos model and the corresponding protocol steps. The situation is as follows: On the left side, a client is running on the user's behalf. In order to use the services that are provided by the server on the bottom of the right side, the client has to authenticate to this server.

In this situation, it is up to the Kerberos KDC to provide the client with credentials that he can use in an authentication exchange. It is important to note that both the client and the server do not initially share a session key. Whenever the client tries to authenticate to the server, he or she relies on the Kerberos KDC to generate a session key and to distribute this key securely to the parties involved.

Kerberos uses tickets to distribute session keys. In general, a ticket is a data record that can be used for authentication. In Kerberos, a ticket is a certificate issued by the Kerberos KDC and encrypted with the server's master key. Among other information, the ticket contains

- The session key that will be used for authentication between the client and the server;

- The name of the principal to whom the session key was issued;

- An expiration time after which the session key is no longer valid.

The ticket is not sent directly to the server, but instead sent to the client who forwards it to the server as part of an authentication exchange. A Kerberos ticket is always encrypted with the server key, known only to the AS and the intended server. Because of this encryption, it is not possible for the client to modify the ticket without detection.

When a user walks up to a workstation and tries to log in, he or she has to enter a username as usual. The login client provides the AS with the username in step (1), and the AS looks up this particular user's entry in the KDC database. The user's password (or the key that is derived from this password) is then used to encrypt a ticket granting ticket (TGT), and the TGT is returned to the client in step (2). The client has to prompt the user to enter his or her password, which is needed to decrypt the TGT. Only if the key that is derived from the user's password successfully decrypts the TGT, is the user able to log in. Otherwise, login is not permitted.

On the client side, the TGT is saved for future use, namely to obtain tickets that can be used to authenticate to particular network services. The primary purpose of the TGT is thus to provide a single sign-on facility for the users. The user is to enter his or her password only once and is not continually prompted for the password each time he or she requests a service.

Tickets are issued by the TGS that is specified in the TGT that the user (or the client acting on the user's behalf) has originally received. To get a ticket, the client sends a corresponding request to the TGS in step (3). The message includes the name of the requested service, the TGT, and an authenticator. An authenticator is a data record containing information that can be shown to have been recently generated using the session key known only by the client and the requested server. In particular, the authenticator contains the user's name, the client's network address, and the current time. It is encrypted using the session key that was returned in the TGT. The authenticator is a simple mechanism designed to discourage replay attacks. If the TGS considers both the ticket and the authenticator as valid, a ticket is returned for the requested network service in step (4). The client builds another authenticator, and sends it along with the service ticket to the server that provides the network service in step (5). If mutual authentication is required, the server returns an authenticator to the client in step (6).

Note that the Kerberos model as described so far only provides an authentication service. By itself, it provides no information as to whether or not the client is authorized to use the service. In general, there are three possibilities to address authorization within the basic Kerberos model:

1. The Kerberos database could maintain authorization information for each service and issue tickets to authorized users only.

2. A dedicated service could maintain authorization information by keeping access lists for each service and allowing the client to obtain sealed certification of list membership. The client would then present the certification, rather than a Kerberos ticket to the requested service.

3. Each service could maintain its own authorization information, with the optional help of a service that stores access lists and provides certification of list membership.

The Kerberos model is based on the assumption that each service knows best who its users should be and what form of authorization is appropriate for them. Consequently, approach three is used in Kerberos. In Chapters 6 and 7 we will see that the main difference between the Kerberos model and the SESAME and OSF DCE Security Service models is due to the fact that the latter are based on approach two to address authorization.

To simplify the implementation of approach three, Kerberos provides a standard authorization model based on access control lists. A corresponding authorization library package is available for incorporation into any service that finds the model useful. Under this model, the service takes the known and authenticated identity of a client and inquires whether or not that client is a member of a named list.

If all parts of Kerberos work properly, users will not normally be aware that Kerberos authentication is in use. The normal login process obtains and caches an initial TGT, and applications automatically obtain and cache tickets as required. Only when authentication fails will users become aware of the use of Kerberos. The following utility programs support the use of Kerberos:

- If a user needs to refresh his or her tickets, they can use the `kinit` utility program, which will get a new TGT after reading a user password from the keyboard. This utility program is typically combined with the UNIX `login` command.

- The utility program `klist` can be used to to display a list of tickets that are obtained and cached for a particular session.

- The utility program **kdestroy** can be used to destroy all tickets that have been obtained and cached for a particular session. This utility program is typically combined with the UNIX **logout** command.

- The utility program **kpasswd** can be used to to change a Kerberos password.

In general, network applications must be modified to use Kerberos for authentication, and Kerberos-aware applications are said to be *Kerberized*. Kerberizing a network application is notably the most difficult part of installing Kerberos.

Fortunately, the MIT reference implementations of Kerberos include versions of popular network applications, such as **telnet** and the Berkeley r-tools, with support of Kerberos already added. Other applications have been Kerberized by vendors and are included in their supported products, too. The availability of Kerberized applications has improved with time, and is expected to improve further. However, a site would still have to arrange itself to add Kerberos support to any application developed in-house.

It is generally necessary to modify the client/server protocol when Kerberizing an application unless the protocol designers have already made provisions for an authentication exchange. The application program must generate and send a Kerberos application request to the application server during the protocol initialization phase, and the server must verify the Kerberos authentication information accordingly. The request must be transmitted within the client/server protocol, and the Kerberos library must provide routines to generate and verify these messages.

More recent implementations of Kerberos provide an application programming interface (API) that conforms to the generic security service application programming interface (GSS-API) specified by the common authentication technology (CAT) working group (WG) of the Internet Engineering Task Force (IETF). The GSS-API is described in Appendix A. In short, it provides a standard API which is authentication mechanism independent. This allows the application programmer to design an application and corresponding protocol that can use alternative authentication mechanisms and technologies, including Kerberos, for example. The use of the GSS-API in application programming is thus highly recommended wherever possible. However, it is only fair to mention that the GSS-API is a generic authentication interface that does not support all of the functionality provided by the current versions of Kerberos.

2.3   CRYPTOGRAPHIC PROTOCOLS

In this section we describe the cryptographic protocols that Kerberos implements. We begin with a brief description of the Needham-Schroeder protocol, and continue with the protocols that are actually used in Kerberos V4 and V5. Finally, we have a closer look at interrealm authentication.

2.3.1   Needham-Schroeder Protocol

Kerberos is based on authentication and key distribution protocols originally proposed by Needham and Schroeder [9,10][3]. The protocols assume the existence of a trusted third party that represents and acts as an *authentication server* (AS). If the AS shares a secret key with every principal, two arbitrary principals A and B can use the AS to mutually authenticate each other, and to be provided with a session key K_{ab} accordingly. The first Needham-Schroeder protocol can be formalized as follows:

$$
\begin{aligned}
1 : A &\longrightarrow AS : A, B, N \\
2 : AS &\longrightarrow A : \{N, B, K_{ab}, \{K_{ab}, A\}K_B\}K_A \\
3 : A &\longrightarrow B : \{K_{ab}, A\}K_B \\
4 : B &\longrightarrow A : \{N_b\}K_{ab} \\
5 : A &\longrightarrow B : \{N_b - 1\}K_{ab}
\end{aligned}
$$

The protocol opens with A communicating in clear to the AS in step (1) his claimed identity and the identity of the desired correspondent B, as well as a nonce N. Upon receiving this message, the AS looks up the secret keys of A and B, namely K_A and K_B, and randomly selects a session key K_{ab} to be shared between A and B. In step (2), the AS returns $\{N, B, K_{ab}, \{K_{ab}, A\}K_B\}K_A$ to A. Note that this message is encrypted with K_A. Consequently, only A will be able to decrypt it, and to extract N, B, K_{ab}, and $\{K_{ab}, A\}K_B$ accordingly. A can check the presence of the nonce N, and the intended recipient's name B, in order to verify that the message really is a reply by the AS to the current enquiry. A remembers K_{ab}, and forwards $\{K_{ab}, A\}K_B$ to B in step (3). Note that $\{K_{ab}, A\}K_B$ is encrypted with K_B, which is the secret key of B; only B will be able to decrypt the message and to

---

[3]Note that in their first paper, Needham and Schroeder propose three protocols; two of which use secret key cryptography, and the other uses public key cryptography.

extract the session key K_{ab} accordingly. By doing so, B can also learn the identity of the intended correspondent A, as authenticated by the AS.

At this point, A knows that any communication he receives encrypted with K_{ab} must have originated with B, and that any communication he emits encrypted with K_{ab} will be understood only by B. This is true because the only messages containing K_{ab} that have been sent so far are tied to A's and B's secret keys. Consequently, the same is true for B. It is important, however, to make sure that no part of the protocol exchange or ensuring conversation is being replayed by an attacker from a recording of a previous protocol run between A and B. With regard to this problem the positions of A and B slightly differ:

- On the one hand, A is aware that he has not used K_{ab} before and therefore has no reason to fear that material encrypted with this key is other than a legitimate response from B.

- On the other hand, B's position is not so good. Unless B remembers all keys previously used by A in order to check that K_{ab} is new, B is unclear that the message received in step (3) and the subsequent messages supposedly from A are not being replayed.

To protect against replay attacks, B has to randomly select a nonce N_b, encrypt it with K_{ab}, and challenge A with the resulting ciphertext in step (4). A has to respond with the decremented and reencrypted nonce in step (5). If the response is satisfactorily received by B, then the mutual confidence is sufficient to enable communication, encrypted with K_{ab}, to begin.

The first Needham-Schroeder protocol consists of five steps. This number can be reduced to three by A's keeping, for regular communication partners, a cache of items of the form $B : K_{ab}, \{K_{ab}, A\}K_B$, thus eliminating steps (1) and (2). Note however that, if such authenticators are cached, changes are needed to the protocol. With caching, the same K_{ab} is being reused again and again, so the conversation handshakes need to be two-way, for example, by replacing steps (3) and (4). The corresponding second Needham-Schroeder protocol can then be formalized as follows:

$$
\begin{aligned}
1 &: A &\longrightarrow& AS &:& A, B, N \\
2 &: AS &\longrightarrow& A &:& \{N, B, K_{ab}, \{K_{ab}, A\}K_B\}K_A \\
3 &: A &\longrightarrow& B &:& \{K_{ab}, A\}K_B, \{N_a\}K_{ab} \\
4 &: B &\longrightarrow& A &:& \{N_a - 1, N_b\}K_{ab} \\
5 &: A &\longrightarrow& B &:& \{N_b - 1\}K_{ab}
\end{aligned}
$$

One major vulnerability of both versions of the Needham-Schroeder protocol is due to the fact that an intruder C who is able to eavesdrop on the message flow can launch an off-line attack on K_{ab}. If C determines a session key K'_{ab} that has been used somewhen in the past, C can impersonate A. As a matter of fact, C can replay the corresponding ticket together with a nonce encrypted with K'_{ab} in step (3). B would challenge A with a nonce in step (4), and because C knows K'_{ab}, C could correctly respond in step (5). The subtle weakness that underlies this vulnerability is due to the fact that the message sent in step (3) contains no information for B to verify its freshness. As a matter of fact, only the AS and A know whether K_{ab} is fresh. This weakness was first discovered by Denning and Sacco [11]. As a possible solution, they have proposed to replace nonces with timestamps, and to use the following protocol instead:

$$
\begin{aligned}
&1 : A \quad \longrightarrow \quad AS : A, B \\
&2 : AS \quad \longrightarrow \quad A \quad : \{B, K_{ab}, T, \{K_{ab}, A, T\}K_B\}K_A \\
&3 : A \quad \longrightarrow \quad B \quad : \{K_{ab}, A, T\}K_B \\
&4 : B \quad \longrightarrow \quad A \quad : \{N_b\}K_{ab} \\
&5 : A \quad \longrightarrow \quad B \quad : \{N_b - 1\}K_{ab}
\end{aligned}
$$

The protocols are more alike than they are different. In the Denning-Sacco protocol, A sends A and B to the AS in step (1), and the AS returns $\{B, K_{ab}, T, \{K_{ab}, A, T\}K_B\}K_A$ to A in step (2). In this case, T represents a timestamp. Again, the message is encrypted with K_A, the secret key of A. A can decrypt the message, and extract B, K_{ab}, T, and $\{K_{ab}, A, T\}K_B$ accordingly. A validates T, and if the timestamp is valid, forwards the ticket $\{K_{ab}, A, T\}K_B$ to B in step (3). B can decrypt the ticket, and extract K_{ab}, A, and T accordingly. B can also validate the timestamp T. If B considers T as being fresh, B selects another nonce N_b, encrypts it with K_{ab}, and returns $\{N_b\}K_{ab}$ to A in step (4). It is finally up to A to decrypt N_b, decrement it, reencrypt it with the same session key, and return $\{N_b - 1\}K_{ab}$ to B in step (5).

Note that in the Denning-Sacco protocol, a timestamp T is used to guarantee the freshness of the messages sent by the AS. A and B can verify whether the messages that they receive in steps (2) and (3) are being replayed by simply comparing them with their local time. If the timestamps are considered fresh, the corresponding messages are accepted, too. However, there are two problems related to the introduction of timestamps:

- First, the use of timestamps requires globally synchronized clocks;

- Second, the definition of acceptable time intervals is a difficult task.

Both problems are not independent, and both problems have quite recently created a new area of research [12,13]. Let's have a closer look at the Kerberos V4 and V5 protocols next.

2.3.2   Kerberos V4

The protocol used in Kerberos V4 is based in part on the Needham-Schroeder protocol(s), with some changes to support the needs of the computing and networking environment for which it had originally been developed. Among these changes are

- The use of timestamps as proposed by Denning and Sacco;
- The addition of a ticket granting service to support subsequent authentication without having the user to reenter his or her password;
- A different approach for interrealm authentication.

Having Figure 2.1 in mind, the Kerberos V4 protocol steps can be formalized as follows:

$$
\begin{array}{llll}
1: \text{C} & \longrightarrow & \text{AS} & : U, TGS, T, L \\
2: \text{AS} & \longrightarrow & \text{C} & : \{K, N, T_{c,tgs}\}K_U \\
3: \text{C} & \longrightarrow & \text{TGS} & : S, N, T_{c,tgs}, A_{c,tgs} \\
4: \text{TGS} & \longrightarrow & \text{C} & : \{T_{c,s}, K'\}K \\
5: \text{C} & \longrightarrow & \text{S} & : T_{c,s}, A_{c,s} \\
6: \text{S} & \longrightarrow & \text{C} & : \{T+1\}K'
\end{array}
$$

In this protocol description, the term $T_{c,tgs} = \{U, C, TGS, T, L, K\}K_{TGS}$ is used to refer to a TGT that is issued by the AS to be used by a client C to authenticate to a TGS, and to request a ticket accordingly. Similarly, the term $T_{c,s} = \{U, C, S, T', L', K'\}K_S$ is used to refer to a ticket that has been issued by the TGS to be used by C to authenticate to a server S. In both expressions, T and T' are used to refer to timestamps, and L and L' are used to refer to the ticket lifetimes. A timestamp represents the number of seconds since 00:00:00 GMT, January 1, 1970, and is coded in four bytes. This is a common representation of time in a UNIX system. Similarly, a lifetime specifies the ticket's lifetime in units of five minutes, and is coded in one byte. Therefore the maximum lifetime that can be expressed in Kerberos V4 is a little over 21 hours.

In addition to that, the terms $A_{c,tgs} = \{C,T\}K$ and $A_{c,s} = \{C,T'\}K'$ are used to refer to authenticators for $T_{c,tgs}$ and $T_{c,s}$ respectively. An authenticator has already been introduced as being a data record containing information that can be shown to have been recently generated using the session key known only by the client and the requested server.

The six steps of the Kerberos protocol can be grouped in three exchanges:

- The *AS exchange* between the client and the AS (steps 1 and 2).

- The *TGS exchange* between the client and the TGS (steps 3 and 4).

- The *AP exchange* between the client and the application server (steps 5 and 6).

These exchanges are discussed next.

The AS Exchange

The AS exchange of the Kerberos V4 protocol is illustrated in Figure 2.2. In short, the client C uses a name service to obtain a list of currently available TGS, and selects the one that is nearest in terms of network topology. C then sends a KRB_AS_REQ (Kerberos authentication server request) message to the Kerberos AS in step (1). The message includes the user identifier U, the identifier for the selected TGS, a timestamp T, and a desired lifetime L for the TGT.

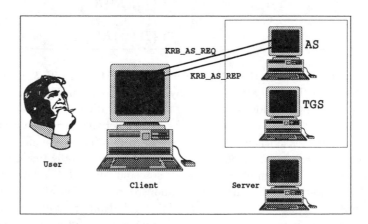

Figure 2.2   The AS exchange.

After having received the KRB_AS_REQ message, the AS looks up and extracts the secret keys that are associated with U and the TGS. The AS then randomly selects a new session key K, and returns a KRB_AS_REP (Kerberos authentication server reply) message to C in step (2). The message includes K, N, and the TGT $T_{c,tgs} = \{U, C, TGS, T, L, K\}K_{TGS}$. In addition to that, the message is encrypted with K_U.

After having received the KRB_AS_REP message, it is up to C to ask U to enter U's password. As a matter of fact, Kerberos V4 does not prompt the user to enter the password until after C has received the KRB_AS_REP message. This is because Kerberos V4 was very serious in following the generally good security rule of having C know the user's password only for the minimum time possible. But waiting the few seconds to get the KRB_AS_REP message before asking the user for the password really doesn't enhance security significantly, and in fact Kerberos V5 has the user enter the password before C sends the KRB_AS_REQ message. The reason for the designers of Kerberos V5 to change the order was that V5 requires C to prove that it knows the user's password before the AS sends the KRB_AS_REP message, which makes it less easy to obtain a quantity with which to launch an offline password guessing attack.

In Kerberos V4, if U correctly enters the password pwd_U, C can use a publicly known one-way hash function h to compute U's secret key $K_U = h(pwd_U)$. Equipped with this key, C can decrypt $\{K, N, T_{c,tgs}\}K_U$, and extract K, N, and $T_{c,tgs}$ accordingly. If C succeeds, C is subsequently in the possession of a TGT that can be used to request tickets from the TGS.

Note that in a TGT, a lifetime is used like a password expiration time. Limiting the lifetime of a TGT thus limits the amount of damage that can be caused by a compromise of the TGT. In Kerberos, there is generally no possibility to revoke a TGT once it has been issued. Thus, limiting the TGT lifetime implicitly sets a deadline after which the TGT becomes obsolete.

The TGS Exchange

The TGS exchange of the Kerberos V4 protocol is illustrated in Figure 2.3. The message format for the TGS exchange is almost identical to the AS exchange. The primary difference is that encryption and decryption in the TGS exchange does not take place under the user's key K_U, but under the session key K that C now shares with the TGS.

Before initiating a TGS exchange, C must determine in which realm the application server he's going to request a ticket for has been registered. If C does not already possess a TGT for that realm, C must obtain one. This is first attempted by requesting a TGT for the destination realm from the local Kerberos server (using the KRB_TGS_REQ message recursively). The Kerberos server may return a TGT for the desired realm, in which case C can proceed. Alternatively, the Kerberos server may also return a TGT for a realm which is closer to the desired realm, in which case this step must be repeated with a Kerberos server in the realm specified in the returned TGT. If neither are returned, the request must be retried with a Kerberos server for a realm higher in the hierarchy. This request will itself require a TGT for the higher realm, which must be obtained by recursively applying these directions. Once the client obtains a TGT for the appropriate realm, it determines which Kerberos servers serve that realm, and contacts one. The list might be obtained through a configuration file or a corresponding network service. The issues involved in interrealm authentication are further discussed in Section 2.3.4.

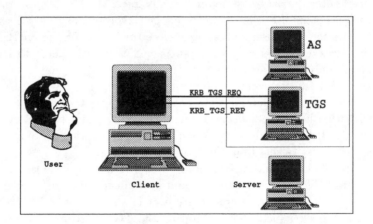

Figure 2.3   The TGS exchange.

In step (3), C sends a KRB_TGS_REQ (Kerberos ticket granting server request) message to the TGS. The message includes S, N, $T_{c,tgs}$, and an authenticator $A_{c,tgs} = \{C, T\}K$, with T being a timestamp. Note that $T_{c,tgs}$ can have a comparably long lifetime, and could be eavesdropped and replayed. The purpose of the authenticator is thus to show that C holds the secret key, and to thwart this kind of attack. Also note that the use of authenticators generally requires that principals on the network keep reasonably synchronized time. The times can be off by some amount. The allowable time skew is independently set at each server, and therefore some servers may be configured to be fussier than others about times being close.

The allowed time skew is usually set to be accurate within five minutes without undue administrative burden. In practice, that assumption has turned out to be more problematic than expected. Distributed time services, once deployed, make much tighter synchronization possible.

The KRB_TGS_REQ message is processed in a manner similar to the KRB_AS_REQ message, but there are some additional checks to be performed. In step (4), the TGS returns a KRB_TGS_REP message (Kerberos ticket granting server reply) that shares its format with the KRB_AS_REP message. It includes a ticket $T_{c,s}$ for the requested server S, and a new session key K', both encrypted with K. When the KRB_TGS_REP is received by C, it is processed in the same manner as the KRB_AS_REP processing described above. The primary difference is that the ciphertext part of the response must be decrypted with the session key that is shared with the TGS rather than with the user's master key.

It turns out that there is neither functionality nor security gained by having Kerberos require an authenticator as part of the KRB_TGS_REQ message. If someone who didn't know the session key K transmitted $T_{c,tgs}$ to the TGS, the TGS would return a message encrypted with K, which would be of no use to someone who didn't know the session key. The reason the designers of Kerberos did it this way is to make the protocol for talking to the TGS be the same as for talking to the other servers. When talking to other servers, the authenticator does indeed provide security, because it authenticates the knowledge of the corresponding session key.

The AP Exchange

The AP exchange of the Kerberos V4 protocol is illustrated in Figure 2.4. It is used by network applications either to authenticate a client to a server, or to mutually authenticate a client and a server to each other. The client must have already acquired credentials for the server using the AS or TGS exchange.

In step (5), C sends a KRB_AP_REQ (Kerberos Application Request) message to the server S. The message includes $T_{c,s}$, $A_{c,s} = \{C, T'\}K'$, and some additional bookkeeping information. Authentication is based on the server's current time of day, the ticket $T_{c,s}$, and the authenticator $A_{c,s}$.

To make sure that the KRB_AP_REQ message is not a replay of a request recent enough to look current given the time skew, S should keep all timestamps received within the maximum allowable time skew and check that each received timestamp is different from any of the stored values. Any authenticator older than the maximum allowable time skew would be rejected anyway, so there is no need to remember values older than the threshold value. Kerberos V4, however, doesn't bother saving

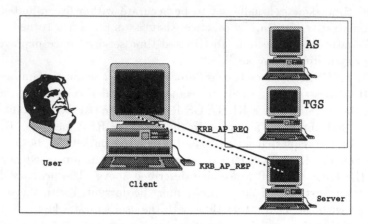

Figure 2.4   The AP exchange.

timestamps. Saving timestamps doesn't help anyway if S is a replicated service in which all the instances of the service use the same master key. The threat of an eavesdropper replaying the authenticator C sent to one instance of S to a different instance of S could have been avoided if Kerberos had done something like put the network layer of the instance of S in the authenticator, too.

If no error occurs, and if mutual authentication is required, S has to return a KRB_AP_REP (Kerberos application reply) message to C in step (6). Again, this message is encrypted with the session key K' that is shared between C and S. Since this key was in the ticket encrypted with the server's secret key, possession of this key is proof that S is the intended principal. More precisely, S has to increment the timestamp included in the KRB_AP_REQ message authenticator, and reencrypt it with K'.

Data Confidentiality and Integrity Services

As described previously, Kerberos provides authentication services. However, a by-product of the Kerberos authentication protocol is the exchange of a session key K' that is shared between the client and the server. This key can subsequently be used by the application to protect the confidentiality and integrity of communications. As a matter of fact, the Kerberos system provides two message types, namely

- The KRB_PRIV message to protect the confidentiality of communications;

- The KRB_SAFE message to protect the integrity of communications.

In spite of these system provided message types, an application is free to use any method that is better suited to the particular data that are transmitted. We are not going to further describe the format of these message types.

Problems of Kerberos

The use of Kerberos significantly improves the security of a network application by making it more difficult for an attacker to impersonate another user. However, Kerberos is not a cure for all network security problems, and Kerberos has its own problems, too. Some limitations and weaknesses of Kerberos V4 were first described by Bellovin and Merritt in [14], and later discussed by Kohl, Neuman, and Ts'o in [15]. We are going to summarize the results of these studies in terms of environmental shortcomings and technical deficiencies next.

Environmental shortcomings: Kerberos V4 was developed primarily for the computing and network environment of the Project Athena, and as such in some areas it makes assumptions and takes approaches that are not always appropriate. The following points can be considered as environmental shortcomings:

- *Cryptosystem dependence:* The MIT reference implementation of Kerberos V4 uses DES to encrypt messages. However, the export of DES from the U.S. is restricted by the government, making truly widespread use of Kerberos V4 rather difficult.

- *Internet protocol dependence:* Kerberos V4 requires the use of Internet Protocol (IP) addresses, which makes it unsuitable for some environments.

- *Message byte ordering:* In Kerberos V4, the sending host encodes multibyte values in network messages in its own natural byte order. It is up to the receiver to convert this byte order into its own native order. While this makes communication between two hosts with the same byte order simple, it does not follow established conventions and will preclude interoperability of a machine with an unusual byte order that is not understood by the receiver.

- *Ticket lifetime:* It has already been mentioned previously that the maximum lifetime that can be expressed in a Kerberos V4 ticket is a little more than 21 hours. This limit has been seen as a major shortcoming of Kerberos V4, since it prevents giving tickets to long-running batch jobs.

- *Authentication forwarding:* Kerberos V4 has no provision for allowing tickets issued to a client on one host to be forwarded to another host, or to be used by another client. Support for this might be useful if an intermediate server needs to access some resource with the rights of the client, or if a user logs into another host on the network and wishes to pursue activities there with the privileges and authentication available on the originating host.

- *Principal naming:* In Kerberos V4, principals are named with three components: name, instance, and realm, each of which may be up to 40 characters long. These sizes, however, have turned out to be too short for some applications and installation environments.

- *Interrealm authentication:* Kerberos V4 allows realms to cooperate by having them share a secret key. A client can obtain tickets for services from a foreign realm's KDC by first obtaining a TGT for the foreign realm from its local KDC and then using that TGT to obtain a ticket for the foreign application server. This pairwise key exchange makes interrealm ticket requests and verification easy to implement, but requires n^2 keys to interconnect n realms. Even with only few cooperating realms, the assignment and management of these many interrealm keys is an expensive task. We discuss the issues of interrealm authentication and key distribution in Section 2.3.4.

Technical Deficiencies: In addition to the environmental shortcomings discussed so far, Kerberos V4 and its reference implementation from MIT also have some technical deficiencies to deal with:

- *Double encryption:* In Kerberos V4, the TGT issued by the AS is encrypted twice when returned to the client, and only once when sent to the TGS. In general, there is no need to encrypt a ticket twice, and doing so can even be a waste of processing power if encryption is computationally intensive.

- *PCBC encryption:* Kerberos V4 uses DES in a nonstandardized version of the CBC mode, namely the plain and cipher block chaining (PCBC) mode. In PCBC mode, a plaintext block P_{i+1} is XOR'ed with both the plaintext P_i and ciphertext C_i before encryption. This mode has the property that modifying a ciphertext block C_i results in garbling of all decrypted plaintext blocks starting with P_i all the way to the end. Kerberos V4 puts some recognizable data at the end of a message that it will encrypt so that it can recognize whether the final block decrypts properly. The assumption is that if the final block decrypts properly, then the data has not been tampered with between the time it was transmitted by the source and received by the destination. However, using DES in PCBC mode and checking the contents of the final decrypted block does not guarantee that Kerberos will be able to detect message corruption. For example, if an intruder is able to interchange two adjacent blocks, PCBC resynchronizes after those two blocks, and the final block will decrypt properly.

- *Message authentication:* Similarly, instead of using DES in CBC mode for integrity protection, Kerberos V4 uses a non standardized checksum algorithm. The idea is to compute a checksum on the session key concatenated with the message, and to transmit both the message and the checksum to the message recipient. The Kerberos V4 checksum algorithm is neither documented nor published. However, nobody has demonstrated the ability to break the algorithm so far, maybe because it has not been widely deployed for applications in which the payoff for breaking the scheme was worth the effort. In general, the fact that an algorithm has not been broken so far, is a weak evidence of its security.

- *Authenticators and replay detection:* Kerberos V4 uses an encrypted timestamp to verify the freshness of messages sent to the servers, and to prevent an intruder from staging a successful replay attack. If an authenticator containing the timestamp is out of date or is being replayed, the application server rejects the authentication. However, maintaining a list of unexpired authenticators that have already been used is hard to implement properly.

Kerberos V5 had evolved over years before it was specified in RFC 1510. Most of the concerns itemized above have been addressed in Kerberos V5 [15].

2.3.3   Kerberos V5

In this subsection, we focus on Kerberos V5 in general, and the main differences to Kerberos V4 in particular. The following changes have been incorporated into Kerberos V5:

- *Principal identifiers:* In Kerberos V5, principal identifiers consist of two parts: a realm name and a remainder. The realm name is separate to facilitate easy implementation of realm traversal routines and realm-sensitive access checks. The remainder is a sequence of however many components are needed to name the principal. Note that a Kerberos V4 principal identifier is just a two-component remainder in Kerberos V5.

- *Use of encryption:* To improve the modularity of Kerberos, the use of encryption has been separated into distinct software modules that can be replaced or removed by programmers at will. When encryption is used in a protocol message, the corresponding ciphertext is tagged with a type identifier so that the recipient can identify the appropriate decryption algorithm necessary to interpret the message. Each encryption algorithm is responsible for providing sufficient integrity protection for the plaintext so that the receiver can verify that the ciphertext was not altered in transit. If the encryption algorithm does not have such properties, it can be augmented by including a checksum in the plaintext before encryption. By doing this, the PCBC mode of DES has been discarded and replaced by the standard CBC mode with an embedded checksum over the plaintext.

- *Network addresses:* When network addresses appear in Kerberos V5 protocol messages, they are similarly tagged with a type and length field so the recipient can interpret them properly. If a host supports multiple network protocols or has multiple addresses of a single type, all types and all addresses can be provided in a ticket.

- *Message encoding:* In Kerberos V5, protocol messages are described using the abstract syntax notation 1 (ASN.1) syntax, and encoded according to the basic encoding rules (BER). This avoids the problem of independently specifying the encoding for multibyte quantities as was done in Kerberos V4. It makes the protocol description look quite different from V4, but it is primarily the presentation of the message fields that changes; the essence of the Kerberos protocol basically remains the same.

- *Ticket format:* The Kerberos V5 ticket has an expanded format to accommodate the required changes from V4. It is split into two parts, one encrypted and the other not. The server's name in the ticket is plaintext since a server with multiple identities, as for example an interrealm TGS, may need the name to select a key with which to decrypt the remainder of the ticket. As a matter of fact, the name of the server is bookkeeping information only and its protection is not necessary for secure authentication. Everything else remains encrypted. In addition to this change, the ticket lifetime is encoded as a starting time and an expiration time (rather than a specific lifetime field), affording nearly limitless ticket lifetimes. The new ticket also contains a flags field and some related fields to enable new features described below.

- *Interrealm support:* In Kerberos V5, realms may cooperate through a hierarchy based on the name of the realm. A source realm is interoperable with a destination realm if it shares an interrealm key directly with the destination realm, or if it shares a key with an intermediate realm that is itself interoperable with the destination realm. Each realm exchanges a different pair of interrealm keys with its parent node and each child. These keys are used in a secret key cryptosystem to obtain tickets for each successive realm along an authentication path.

In addition to that, several new features are supported by Kerberos V5. For example, the flags field mentioned above allows greater flexibility in the use of Kerberos V5 tickets than is available in V4. Each ticket issued by the AS using the initial AS exchange is flagged as such. This allows servers, such as a password changing server, to require that a client present a ticket obtained by direct use of the client's secret key instead of one obtained using a TGT. Such a requirement prevents an attacker from walking up to an unattended but logged in workstation and changing another user's password.

In Kerberos V5, tickets may also be issued as renewable with two expiration times, one for a time in the near future, and one later. The ticket expires as usual at the earlier time, but if it is presented to the TGS in a renewal request before this earlier expiration time, a replacement ticket may be returned that is valid for an additional period of time. However, a TGS will not renew a ticket beyond the second expiration time indicated in the ticket. This mechanism has the advantage that although credentials can be used for long periods of time, the TGS may refuse to renew tickets that are reported as stolen and thereby thwart their continued use.

A similar mechanism is available to assist authentication during batch processing. A ticket issued as postdated and invalid will not be valid until its postdated starting time passes and it is replaced with a validated ticket. The client validates the ticket by presenting it to the TGS as described above for renewable tickets.

Authentication forwarding can be implemented by contacting the TGS with an additional TGS exchange and requesting a ticket valid for a different set of network addresses than the TGT used in the request. The TGS will not issue such tickets unless the presented TGT has a flag set indicating that this is a permissible use of the ticket. When the entity on the remote host is granted only limited rights to use the authentication, the forwarded credentials are referred to as a proxy. A proxy is handled similarly to a forwarded ticket, except that a new proxy ticket will not be issued for a TGS; it will only be issued for an application server.

Kerberos is concerned primarily with authentication. It is not directly concerned with related security services, such as authorization and accounting. To support the implementation of these security services, Kerberos V5 provides a mechanism for the tamper-proof transmission of authorization and accounting information as part of a ticket. This information may restrict the use of a ticket. The encoding of the corresponding restriction is not a concern of the Kerberos protocol, but is instead defined by the authorization and accounting mechanisms in use. The restrictions are coded in the authorization data field of a ticket.

When a ticket is requested, restrictions are specified and sent to the TGS where they are inserted into the ticket, encrypted, and protected from tampering. In the protocol's most general form, a client requests that the KDC include or add such data to a new ticket. The TGS does not remove any authorization data from a TGT, but copies it into every new ticket, and also adds any requested additional authorization data. Upon decryption of a ticket, the authorization data is available to the application server, too. While Kerberos makes no interpretation of the data, the application server is expected to use the authorization data to restrict the client's access to the resource specified in the ticket.

Among other uses, the authorization data field can also be used in a proxy ticket to create a capability. The client requesting the proxy ticket from a TGS specifies authorization restrictions in the authorization data field, then securely transmits the proxy and session key to another party, which uses the ticket to obtain limited service from an application server. As discussed in Chapter 7, the Open Software Foundation's distributed computing environment (OSF DCE) uses the authorization data field to place privilege attribute certificates (PACs).

In an effort to complicate the theft of passwords, the Kerberos V5 protocol provides a preauthentication data field to support password alternatives, such as one-time passwords generated by handheld authenticators. In the initial AS exchange, the preauthentication data field can be used to alter the key in which the reply is encrypted, too. This makes a stolen password useless since fresh information from a physical device is needed to decrypt a response.

In Kerberos V5, tickets are cached on the client side. To avoid problems caused by the reuse of a session keys across multiple connections, a client can choose a new key for a session, and this key is called a *subsession key*. A subsession key is discarded once the corresponding session is closed.

As discussed in the previous subsection, Kerberos provides two message formats for applications to protect communications. The KRB_SAFE message uses a cryptographic checksum to ensure data integrity, whereas the KRB_PRIV message uses encryption to ensure data confidentiality. In Kerberos V4, these messages include as control information a timestamp and the sender's network address. With V5, an application may elect to use a timestamp as before, or a sequence number. If a timestamp is used, then the receiver must record the known timestamps to avoid replay attacks. Otherwise, if a sequence number is used, then the receiver must verify that the messages arrive in proper order without any gap. In general, there are situations where one choice makes an application simpler to implement.

Again, having Figure 2.1 in mind, the Kerberos V5 protocol steps can be formalized as follows:

$$
\begin{array}{llll}
1 : C & \longrightarrow & AS & : U, TGS, L_1, N_1 \\
2 : AS & \longrightarrow & C & : U, T_{c,tgs}, \{TGS, K, T_{start}, T_{expire}, N_1\}K_U \\
3 : C & \longrightarrow & TGS & : S, L_2, N_2, T_{c,tgs}, A_{c,tgs} \\
4 : TGS & \longrightarrow & C & : U, T_{c,s}, \{S, K', T'_{start}, T'_{expire}, N_2\}K \\
5 : C & \longrightarrow & S & : T_{c,s}, A_{c,s} \\
6 : S & \longrightarrow & C & : \{T'\}K'
\end{array}
$$

Analogous to Kerberos V4, $T_{c,tgs}$ and $T_{c,s}$ are used to refer to a TGT and a ticket, respectively, and $A_{c,tgs}$ and $A_{c,s}$ are used to refer to the corresponding authenticators.

In step (1), C selects a TGS, and sends a corresponding KRB_AS_REQ message to the Kerberos AS. The message includes the user identifier U, the identifier of the selected TGS, a requested lifespan L_1 for the TGT, and a nonce N_1. In addition to that, the message may specify a number of options, such as

- If preauthentication is to be performed;
- If the requested ticket is to be renewable, proxiable, or forwardable;
- If it should be postdated or allow postdating of derivative tickets;
- If a renewable ticket will be accepted instead of a nonrenewable ticket if the requested ticket expiration date cannot be satisfied by a nonrenewable ticket.

After having received the KRB_AS_REQ message, the AS looks up and extracts the secret keys for U and the TGS. If required, the AS preauthenticates the request, and if preauthentication fails, a corresponding error message is returned to C. Otherwise, the AS randomly selects a new session key K, and returns a KRB_AS_REP message to C in step (2). The message includes U, a TGT $T_{c,tgs} = \{U, C, TGS, K, T_{start}, T_{expire}\}K_{tgs}$, and $\{TGS, K, T_{start}, T_{expire}, N_1\}K_U$. The TGT's start and expiration times T_{start} and T_{expire} are set in accordance with the realm's security policy in a way that possibly fits the specified lifespan L_1 in the KRB_AS_REQ message.

After having received the KRB_AS_REP message, C applies the one-way hash function h to the user-provided password pwd_U to compute the user's master key $K_U = h(pwd_U)$. Equipped with this key, C can decrypt $\{TGS, K, T_{start}, T_{expire}\}K_U$, and extract TGS, K, T_{start} and T_{expire} accordingly. C is now in the possession of a TGT that is valid from T_{start} to T_{expire}. He can use this TGT to request tickets from the TGS.

A TGS exchange is initiated whenever C wants to obtain a ticket for a server, renew or validate an existing ticket, or even obtain a proxy ticket. At least in the first case, the client must already have acquired a TGT using the AS exchange. In step (3), C sends a KRB_TGS_REQ message to the TGS. Again, the message includes information authenticating the client plus a request for credentials. The authentication information consists of both the TGT $T_{c,tgs}$, and a corresponding authenticator $A_{c,tgs} = \{C, T\}K$ that C generates with a timestamp T and the session key K. In step (4), the TGS returns a KRB_TGS_REP message that includes a ticket $T_{c,s} = \{U, C, S, K', T'_{start}, T'_{expire}\}K_s$ for the requested server S, as well as $\{S, K', T'_{start}, T'_{expire}\}K$.

Again, an AP exchange is used either to authenticate a client to a server or to mutually authenticate a client and a server to each other. In step (5), C sends a KRB_AP_REQ message to the server S. The message contains the ticket $T_{c,s}$, and a corresponding authenticator $A_{c,s} = \{C, T'\}K'$, together with some bookkeeping information. Authentication is based on the server's current time of day, the authenticator, and the ticket. If no error occurs, and if mutual authentication is required, S returns a KRB_AP_REP message in step (6). This message includes the timestamp T', encrypted with the session key K' that S now shares with C.

2.3.4   Interrealm Authentication

In general, a network environment may consist of several organizations, such as companies in competition with each other, government agencies, financial institutions, or universities. In such an environment, it would be hard to find an entity that everyone would trust to run and manage a Kerberos KDC. The point is that within the Kerberos model, whoever runs and manages the KDC can access every user's master key, and therefore access everything that any user can access. Even if there were an entity everyone was willing to trust, this is not enough. Everyone must also trust the physical controls around every replica of the KDC, and there would have to be widely dispersed replicas to ensure availability and convenience. Compromise of any replica, no matter how obscurely placed it was, would yield every principal's keys. Furthermore, that highly trusted entity would also be a very busy one, having to process all instances of users and services joining and leaving the network environment.

For this reason, the network environment is divided into realms, and each realm is assumed to run its own KDC. There can be multiple KDCs in a realm, but they would be equivalent, have the same KDC master key, and have the same database entries for principals. Two KDCs in different realms, however, would have different KDC master keys and totally different principal's master key databases, since they would be responsible for a different set of principals.

Kerberos has been designed to operate across organizational boundaries, and a client in one realm can, in principle, authenticate to a server in another realm. In Kerberos, an authentication across realm boundaries is called an *interrealm authentication*.

An *interrealm key* is a secret key that is shared between the KDCs of two Kerberos realms. By establishing interrealm keys, the administrators of Kerberos realms can allow a client authenticated in one realm to use its authentication remotely. The exchange of interrealm keys registers the TGS of each realm as a principal in the other realm. A client is then able to obtain a TGT for the remote realm's TGS from its local realm. When that TGT is used, the remote TGS uses the interrealm key to decrypt the TGT, and is thus certain that it was issued by the client's TGS. Tickets issued by the remote TGS will indicate to a service that the client was authenticated from another realm.

A realm is said to communicate with another realm if the two realms share an interrealm key, or if the local realm shares an interrealm key with an intermediate realm that communicates with the remote realm. In the Kerberos terminology, an authentication path refers to a sequence of intermediate realms that are transited in the authentication process when communicating from one realm to another.

It has already been mentioned that with Kerberos V4, it was necessary for an AS to register with every other realm with which interrealm authentication is required. This doesn't scale, and complete interconnection requires the exchange of n^2 keys, with n being the total number of realms.

In contrast, Kerberos V5 supports multihop interrealm authentication, allowing keys to be shared hierarchically. With Kerberos V5, each realm shares a key with its children and parent realms. If an interrealm key is not directly shared by two realms, the hierarchical organization allows an authentication path to be established. If a hierarchical organization is not used, it may be necessary to consult some database in order to construct an authentication path between realms. Although realms are typically hierarchical, intermediate realms may be bypassed to achieve interrealm authentication through alternate authentication paths. These might be established to make communication between two realms more efficient. It is important for the a requested service to know which realms were transited when deciding how much faith to place in the authentication process as a whole. To facilitate this decision, a field in each ticket lists the sequence of transited realms, omitting the source and destination realms. Realm names are listed separated by commas. Since the list of transited realms might get large, Kerberos permits various abbreviations.

The hierarchical organization of realms in Kerberos V5 is thus similar to the hierarchical organization of CAs in public key cryptography. As with the certification hierarchy, the utility of the authentication infrastructure supporting authentication between parties not previously known to one another depends in part on the availability of authentication servers for realms near the top of the hierarchy. Unfortunately, political and legal ambiguity has the potential to slow down the establishment of these realms.

2.4   DISCUSSION

By describing Kerberos in corresponding publications and making the source code publicly available, the Kerberos designers and implementors at MIT have made a commendable effort to encourage a public system review. It is important to note that Kerberos is still associated with the original Needham-Schroeder protocol, although there are at least two points to mention that have significantly improved the protocol:

1. The use of authenticators allows tickets to be issued for a longer period of time than was originally proposed by Denning and Sacco [11].

2. The use of TGSs allows an easy and efficient way to provide a single sign-on.

Environmental shortcomings and technical deficiencies of Kerberos V4 have been discussed in subsection 2.3.2. Some of these shortcomings and deficiencies have led to the current design of Kerberos V5, whereas others haven't been addressed so far. As a matter of fact, there are some problems related to the Kerberos model that are equally valid for Kerberos V4 and V5.

For example, it is often critiziced that Kerberos uses untrusted workstations that are not reset between individual sessions. This means that the ability of an attacker to deploy Trojan horses and other malicious software attacks to gain access is not adequately dealt with.

Another point that is often made is related to the fact that the system was primarily designed for user-to-host authentication, and not for user-to-user or host-to-host authentication. That was reasonable in the Athena network environment of anonymous, dataless workstations, and large-scale file and mail servers. However, it might be a poor match for environments in which hosts have identities of their own and need to access resources such as remotely mounted file systems on their own behalf. To do so within the Kerberos model would require that hosts maintain secret keys. Unfortunately, computer systems are notoriously poor at keeping keys secret.

A related issue has to do with the ticket and session cache. Again, multiuser computer systems are not good at keeping secrets. Anyone who can read a cached session key can use it to impersonate the legitimate user. The corresponding ticket can be picked up by eavesdropping on the network, or by obtaining privileged status on the host. With the emerging use of multiuser computer systems and workstations, this lack of host security is assumed to become a more serious problem for Kerberos. However, it is only fair to mention that this problem is a more general one, and not necessarily related to Kerberos.

Another more general problem is due to the fact that if a user wants to submit a large batch job to be performed at a later time, the user has to authenticate himself or herself at that time or to store the password in a batch file. Both possibilities are not satisfactory. One possibility to overcome this problem is to extend operating system commands, such as the **at** command in UNIX, with Kerberos-specific features [16].

With regard to technical deficiencies, perhaps the most obvious problem is that Kerberos still relies on well-chosen passwords and the secrecy of them. If an attacker can gain access to another user's password, there is, in general, no way for Kerberos to distinguish between the legitimate user and the attacker. There are two points to make in this respect:

- First, people are known to use poorly chosen passwords that are vulnerable to password guessing and dictionary attacks [17,18,19]. Similarly, all available evidence suggests that forcing people to choose and remember good passwords is unworkable, because such well-chosen passwords are also unmemorable.

- Second, Kerberos is exposed to "verifiable password" attacks. In step (2) of the Kerberos protocol, the AS returns a message to the client that is encrypted with a key derived from the user's password. If an attacker is able to request this message, or is able to grab it with a passive wiretapping attack, he or she can launch an offline password guessing attack. Note that in this case, an offline password guessing attack can be launched simultaneously against all messages that the attacker knows. There is no analogue to the UNIX salt mechanism to urge an attacker to address each account individually.

In principle, "verifiable password" attacks are a special case of a new form of hostile attacks called *verifiable-text attacks*, and that verifiable-text attacks form a superset of known-plaintext attacks. While vulnerabilities to known-plaintext attacks are fairly easy to detect and correct, verifiable-text attacks are, in general, much more subtle and more difficult to avoid. Again, we should point out that "verifiable password"-attacks are only a serious threat if passwords are user-chosen and weak.

Two techniques were independently proposed to make the Kerberos AS exchange resistant against "verifiable password" attacks. One technique was proposed by Lomas, Gong, Saltzer, and Needham [20,21], and the other technique was proposed by Bellovin and Merritt [22,23]. We are not going to discuss the techniques at this point, mainly because they rely on public key cryptography, an approach explicitly rejected for the original Kerberos design.

A somehow related problem of Kerberos V5 is due to the fact that it is not as secure against replay attacks as it could be. Unless the server keeps track of all previously used authenticators within the allowable clock-skew window, an intruder can launch replay attacks. For that matter, if the attacker could fool the host into believing an incorrect time of day, the host could provide a ready supply of postdated authenticators for later abuse. As a matter of fact, Kerberos assumes the system clocks to be loosely synchronized on all hosts. Consequently, a global time must be available to all hosts that use the Kerberos system. A nonce-based protocol that does not require synchronized clocks is proposed in [24] and further discussed in [25]. It might be interesting at this point that the answer of Needham and Schroeder to the vulnerability found by Denning and Sacco was indeed a nonce-based protocol [10]. However, this proposal has not been used in Kerberos V4 or V5.

Perhaps the biggest problem of Kerberos is not even related to its security, but rather to its implementation. Because network services must perform authentication, this means that every network application that makes use of authentication must be modified to use Kerberos. While the modifications are not difficult, they do require source code. The Kerberos distribution comes along with the most common applications already modified, allowing at least these services to make use of authentication. But sites without a UNIX source license are somewhat out of luck. Note that this may change in the future, as several versions of UNIX are scheduled to contain Kerberos by default.

There are several projects going on either to extend the Kerberos protocol to new environments and requirements or to use Kerberos in new applications:

- Examples of the first category are *Charon*,[4] an extension of the Kerberos protocol for secondary networks [26], the integration of one-time passwords with Kerberos [27], or the use of public key cryptography in the initial AS exchange [28].

- An example of the second category is described in [8]. In this new application, Kerberos is used to set up a Pretty Good Privacy (PGP) public key signer service that, in principle, represents an automated introducer for PGP (Zimmermann, 1995a; Zimmermann, 1995b). Note that PGP was chosen for this exemplary application mainly because it has a significant presence in the Internet community, and that a similar Privacy Enhance Mail (PEM) (Kent, 1993) signer service could be created using most of the functions of the PGP signer service.

A new method of adding public key cryptography to Kerberos was recently proposed as *Yaksha*[5] [29]. Yaksha uses as its building block Boyd's generalization of the RSA public key cryptosystem [30]. With regard to digital multisignatures, the generalization suggests the RSA private key k^{-1} to be split into multiple portions $k_1^{-1}, k_2^{-1}, \ldots, k_l^{-1}$, with $k_1^{-1} k_2^{-1} \ldots k_l^{-1} \equiv k^{-1} \bmod \phi(n)$. The ith portion of k^{-1}, namely k_i^{-1}, is given to the ith user, so that all users can jointly sign messages. For example, if there are two users ($l = 2$), then the first user computes $S_1 \equiv M^{k_1^{-1}} \bmod n$, and the second user completes the signature by computing $S \equiv S_1^{k_2^{-1}} \bmod n$. The resulting signature is identical to one signed by the regular RSA private key k^{-1} and can hence be verified in one operation using the corresponding public key k. It has been shown that breaking the RSA multisignature scheme is equivalent to breaking RSA at first place.

The basic idea of Yaksha is to randomly select a RSA public key pair (k_P, k_P^{-1}) during the registration process of principal P, and to use the generalization of the RSA public key cryptosystem to split the private key k_P^{-1} into two portions, namely $k_{P_1}^{-1}$ and $k_{P_2}^{-1}$, with $k_{P_1}^{-1} k_{P_2}^{-1} k_P \equiv 1 (\bmod \phi(n_P))$. If P is a user, then $k_{P_1}^{-1}$ is derived from P's password, and $k_{P_2}^{-1}$ is computed accordingly. At the end of the registration process, P is equipped with $k_{P_1}^{-1}$, and the Yaksha server is equipped with $k_{P_2}^{-1}$. In this case, $k_{P_1}^{-1}$ is a private portion of k_P^{-1} that is known only to P, and $k_{P_2}^{-1}$ is a corresponding private portion of k_P^{-1} that is known exclusively to the Yaksha server.

If P wants to mutually authenticate to the Yaksha server, P reveals knowledge of $k_{P_1}^{-1}$, and the Yaksha server reveals knowledge of $k_{P_2}^{-1}$. To fully take advantage of

---

[4]In Greek mythology, Charon was the ferryman to souls over the river Styx to Hades.

[5]In Hindu mythology, Yakshas are demigods who, among other things, guard the gates of heaven.

public key cryptography, Yaksha assumes certificates for public keys to be stored and distributed by the Yaksha server, too. For principal P, the certificate is digitally signed with the Yaksha server's private key k_Y^{-1}, and the corresponding public key (k_Y, n_Y) is made publicly available.

To avoid having the user's portion of the private key stored on a computer for a lengthy period, Yaksha uses this key in conjunction with the corresponding portion of the Yaksha server to digitally sign a certificate for a temporary delegation key. The client thus randomly selects a public key pair (k_p, k_p^{-1}), and uses these keys to run the Yaksha protocol.

REFERENCES

[1] J.G. Steiner, B.C. Neuman, and J.I. Schiller, "Kerberos: An Authentication Service for Open Network Systems," *in Proceedings of the USENIX UNIX Security Symposium*, USENIX Association, Berkeley, CA, August 1988.

[2] J. Kohl, and B.C. Neuman, "The Kerberos Network Authentication Service," Massachusetts Institute of Technology (MIT), Cambridge, MA, December 1990.

[3] J.I. Schiller, "Secure Distributed Computing," *Scientific American*, November 1994, pp. 72 – 76.

[4] G.A. Champine, D.E. Geer, and W.N. Ruh, "Project Athena as a Distributed Computer System," *IEEE Computer*, Vol. 23, September 1990, pp. 40 – 50.

[5] G.A. Champine, *MIT Project Athena — A Model for Distributed Computing*, Digital Press, 1991.

[6] S.P. Miller, B.C. Neuman, J.I. Schiller, and J.H. Saltzer, "Kerberos Authentication and Authorization System," Massachusetts Institute of Technology (MIT), Cambridge, MA, December 1987, Section E.2.1 of the Project Athena Technical Plan.

[7] J. Kohl, and B.C. Neuman, "The Kerberos Network Authentication Service (V5)," Request for Comments 1510, September 1993.

[8] J.I. Schiller, and D.A. Atkins, "Scaling the Web of Trust: Combining Kerberos and PGP to Provide Large Scale Authentication," *in Proceedings of the Technical Conference on UNIX and Advanced Computing Systems*, USENIX Association, Berkeley, CA, January 1995, pp. 83 – 94.

[9] R.M. Needham, and M.D. Schroeder, "Using Encryption for Authentication in Large Networks of Computers," *Communications of the ACM*, Vol. 21, December 1978, pp. 993 – 999.

[10] R.M. Needham, and M.D. Schroeder, "Authentication Revisited," *ACM Operating Systems Review*, Vol. 21, 1987, p. 7.

[11] D.E. Denning, and G. Sacco, "Timestamps in Key Distribution Protocols," *Communications of the ACM*, Vol. 24, 1981, pp. 533 – 536.

[12] L. Gong, "A Security Risk of Depending on Synchronized Clocks," *ACM Operating Systems Review*, Vol. 26, 1992, pp. 49 – 53.

[13] K.Y. Lam, and T. Beth, "Timely Authentication in Distributed Systems," in Y. Deswarte, G. Eizenberg, and J.J. Quisquater, editors, *ESORICS '92 — European Symposium on Research in Computer Security*, Springer-Verlag, Berlin, November 1992, pp. 293 – 303.

[14] S.M. Bellovin, and M. Merritt, "Limitations of the Kerberos Authentication System," *ACM Computer Communication Review*, Vol. 20, 1990, pp. 119 – 132.

[15] J.T. Kohl, B.C. Neuman, and T.Y. Ts'o, "The Evolution of the Kerberos Authentication System," in F.M.T. Brazier and D. Johansen, editors, *Distributed Open Systems*, IEEE Computer Society Press, Los Alamitos, CA, 1994, pp. 78 – 94.

[16] A.D. Rubin, and P. Honeyman, "Long Running Jobs in an Authenticated Environment," *in Proceedings of the USENIX UNIX Security IV Symposium*, USENIX Association, Berkeley, CA, October 1993, pp. 19 – 28.

[17] R. Morris, and K. Thompson, "Password Security: A Case History," *Communications of the ACM*, Vol. 22, 1979, pp. 594 – 597.

[18] D.C. Feldmeier, and P.R. Karn, "UNIX Password Security — Ten Years Later," in G. Brassard, editor, *Advances in Cryptology — CRYPTO '89*, Springer-Verlag, Berlin, 1990, pp. 44 – 63.

[19] D.V. Klein, "Foiling the Cracker: A Survey of, and Improvements to, Password Security," *in Proceedings of the USENIX UNIX Security II Symposium*, USENIX Association, Berkeley, CA, August 1990, pp. 5 – 14.

[20] T.M.A. Lomas, L. Gong, J.H. Saltzer, and R.M. Needham, "Reducing Risks from Poorly Chosen Keys," *ACM Operating Systems Review*, Vol. 23, 1989, Special Issue — Proceedings of the Twelfth ACM Symposium on Operating Systems Principles, pp. 14 – 18.

[21] L. Gong, T.M.A. Lomas, R.M. Needham, and J.H. Saltzer, "Protecting Poorly Chosen Secrets from Guessing Attacks," *IEEE Journal on Selected Areas in Communications*, Vol. 11, June 1993, pp. 648 – 656.

[22] S.M. Bellovin, and M. Merritt, "Encrypted Key Exchange: Password-Based Protocols Secure Against Dictionary Attacks," *in Proceedings of the IEEE Symposium on Security and Privacy*, IEEE Computer Society Press, Los Alamitos, CA, 1992, pp. 72 – 84.

[23] S.M. Bellovin, and M. Merritt, "Augmented Encrypted Key Exchange," *in Proceedings of the 1st ACM Conference on Communications and Computing Security*, November 1993, pp. 244 – 250.

[24] A. Kehne, J. Schönwälder, and H. Langendörfer, "A Nonce-based Protocol for Multiple Authentication," *ACM Operating Systems Review*, Vol. 26, 1992, pp. 84 – 89.

[25] B.C. Neuman, and S.G. Stubblebine, "A Note on the Use of Timestamps and Nonces," *ACM Operating Systems Review*, Vol. 27, 1993, pp. 10 – 14.

[26] D.A. Atkins, "Charon: Kerberos Extensions For Authentication Over Secondary Networks," Massachusetts Institute of Technology (MIT), Cambridge, MA, May 1993.

[27] B.C. Neuman, and G. Zorn, "Integrating One-time Passwords with Kerberos," Internet Draft, April 1995, work in pogress.

[28] B.C. Neuman, B. Tung, and J. Wray, "Public Key Cryptography for Initial Authentication in Kerberos," Internet Draft, March 1995, work in pogress.

[29] R. Ganesan, "Yaksha: Augmenting Kerberos with Public Key Cryptography," in *Proceedings of the Internet Society. Symposium on Network and Distributed System Security*, February 1995, pp. 132 – 143.

[30] C. Boyd, "Some Applications of Multiple Key Ciphers," in C.G. Günther, editor, *Proceedings of EUROCRYPT '88*, Springer-Verlag, Berlin, 1989, pp. 455 – 467.

Chapter 3

NetSP

In this chapter, we focus on the authentication and key distribution system NetSP (network security program) that has been developed by IBM. The distinguishing feature of NetSP is its use of a keyed one-way hash function instead of a full-fledged cryptosystem. In Section 3.1, we summarize the development of the system, and in Section 3.2 we focus on the cryptographic protocols that NetSP implements. In Section 3.3, we discuss the applicability of the cryptographic protocols outside the scope of NetSP.

3.1 DEVELOPMENT

In general, a *keyed one-way hash function* is a one-way hash function parameterized by a secret key. Such a hash function can be used to add controlled redundancy to information and to protect thus the integrity of the information. The use of keyed one-way hash functions was independently proposed by Cohen to protect the integrity of software [1], and Gong and Tsudik to compute and verify message authentication codes (MACs) [2,3]. There were even some preliminary thoughts about using keyed one-way hash functions to secure messages in the simple network management protocol (SNMP) version 2.

Prior to these proposals, the usual way to compute and verify an MAC was to use a secret key cryptosystem, such as DES, to encrypt a message in the cipher block chaining (CBC) mode, and to use the last ciphertext block as an MAC. The idea of using a keyed one-way hash function for message authentication is to concatenate the message that is to be authenticated with a secret key, and to use a collision-resistant one-way hash function, such as MD4, MD5, or the SHS, to generate an MAC. Various methods can serve as concatenation functions, and the secret prefix, secret suffix, and envelope methods were originally proposed in [3]. However, recent results in cryptographic research have shown that these methods have weaknesses that may be exploited by some sophisticated attacks [4,5].

A substantial advantage of keyed one-way hash functions over techniques that use encryption for message authentication is speed, because one-way hash functions, in general, work much faster than encryption. Another big advantage is that neither the source code nor the design of the resulting implementations are subject to U.S. export controls. Both advantages are very attractive from a manufacturer's or vendor's point of view.

The idea of using keyed one-way hash functions for message authentication, and to use MACs for authentication and key distribution has led to a joint project between the IBM Research Laboratories in Zürich, Switzerland, and the Thomas J. Watson Research Center in Yorktown Heights, New York. The objective of the project was to design a family of minimal, flexible, and scalable authentication and key distribution protocols that could be used in different network environments, as well as to show the resistance of these protocols against specific attacks.

In general, achieving minimal and flexible protocols is desirable because of the prevailing view that security mechanisms are expensive, performance-impairing, and somehow cumbersome. As a matter of fact, this view often results in single users or organizations avoiding, disabling, or bypassing implemented security mechanisms.

Protocol minimality can be expressed in several ways, such as number of messages that must be exchanged during the execution of a protocol, size of each individual message, or number of cryptographic operations. Protocol minimality finally pays off when security features must be retrofitted into existing protocols or applications. If, as is often the case, security features have to be introduced as an afterthought, security parameters must be squeezed into the meager space available (e.g., in packet headers). This point is best illustrated by considering the ongoing discussions within some working groups of the Internet Engineering Task Force (IETF) or the ATM Forum. With regard to scalability, it should be noted that an authentication and key distribution solution, in general, needs to be extensible to large internets comprising many interconnected administration domains.

IBM's resulting family of lightweight authentication and key distribution protocols was first described in [6], and later discussed in [7,8]. The protocols are efficient in terms of message size and computation overhead, and minimal in terms of using cryptographic techniques. In addition to that, the protocols have shown to be resistant to a wide set of attacks known as interleaving attacks. In short, an *interleaving attack* refers to an attack that is based on the attacker's ability to use either legitimate message flows obtained from past executions of a protocol or message flows elicited by the attacker from legitimate parties.

Some of the family's major protocols were prototyped in an authentication and key distribution system named *KryptoKnight*[1] [9]. Because of this prototype's name, the protocol family is also referred to as the *KryptoKnight* or *KK protocols*.

Today, the KK protocols are also used in IBM's network security program (NetSP). NetSP consists of several network security products, such as

- a NetSP secured network gateway (NetSP SNG), and
- a NetSP secured logon coordinator (NetSP SLC).

NetSP SNG is a firewall product, whereas NetSP SLC is a full-fledged authentication and key distribution system. This book is about authentication and key distribution systems, so whenever we talk about NetSP, we implicitly refer to NetSP SLC.

NetSP version 1 (V1) was officially released in January 1994 for the AIX/6000, OS/2, and MS-DOS operating systems. In addition to the TCP/IP protocols for these platforms, NetBIOS was supported on AIX, OS/2, and MS-DOS, and LU 6.2 was supported on AIX and OS/2, too. NetSP V1 provided secured single sign-on to 3270 host applications that use RACF (resource access control facility). In August 1994, NetSP was upgraded to version 1.2[2]. In NetSP V1.2, platforms from the AIX/6000, OS/2, and MS-DOS operating systems are extended to additionally include HP, Sun, and DOS/Windows for client and application server workstations. IPX/SPX is supported on OS/2 and DOS/Windows for authentication servers and clients running on workstations with Novell NetWare. TCP/IP is supported on AIX, OS/2, HP, Sun, and DOS/Windows platforms. Single sign-on support for OS/2 has been extended to LanServer and Novell.

---

[1]http://www.zurich.ibm.com/Technology/Security/extern/kryptoknight
[2]http://www.ibm.com/oi/ann/alet/294502.html

3.2   CRYPTOGRAPHIC PROTOCOLS

In this section, we overview the KK protocols. In particular, we focus on two-party authentication and key distribution, three-party key distribution, interdomain key distribution, and single sign-on protocols.

3.2.1   Two-Party Authentication

The following two-party authentication protocol (2PAP) is at the core of the KK protocols. It specifies a challenge-response protocol that allows two principals A and B to authenticate each other. The 2PAP can be formalized as follows:

$$1 : A \longrightarrow B : N_a$$
$$2 : B \longrightarrow A : N_b, \langle N_a, N_b, B \rangle K_{ba}$$
$$3 : A \longrightarrow B : \langle N_a, N_b \rangle K_{ab}$$

In this protocol description, the originator and recipient of a message are omitted in the message bodies, because they can be derived from the corresponding network addressing information. N_a and N_b are used to refer to nonces that are randomly selected by A and B, respectively. Remember that we have introduced the term $\langle m \rangle K$ to refer to an MAC that is computed from the message m with the secret key K. Consequently, the term $\langle N_a, N_b, B \rangle K_{ba}$ is used to refer to an MAC that is computed from the concatenation of N_a, N_b, and B with the secret key K_{ba}. Similarly, the term $\langle N_a, N_b \rangle K_{ab}$ is used to refer to an MAC that is computed from the concatentaion of N_a and N_b with the secret key K_{ab}. If both MAC functions are implemented with a secret key cryptosystem, then K_{ba} and K_{ab} refer to secret keys that are shared by A and B. In this case, K_{ba} and K_{ab} are typically the same. For example, if DES is used in CBC mode for message authentication, then the term $\langle N_a, N_b, B \rangle K_{ba}$ in fact abbreviates $\{\{\{N_a\}K_{ba} \oplus N_b\}K_{ba} \oplus B\}K_{ba}$, and $\langle N_a, N_b \rangle K_{ab}$ abbreviates $\{\{N_a\}K_{ab} \oplus N_b\}K_{ab}$. But instead of using a full-fledged cryptosystem to compute and verify MACs, one can also use a keyed one-way hash function h as mentioned previously. In this case, $\langle N_a, N_b, B \rangle K_{ba}$ refers to $h(K_{ba}, N_a, N_b, B)$ for the secret prefix method, $h(N_a, N_b, B, K_{ba})$ for the secret suffix method, and $h(K_{ba}, N_a, N_b, B, K_{ba})$ for the envelope method. Similarly, $\langle N_a, N_b \rangle K_{ab}$ refers to $h(K_{ab}, N_a, N_b)$ for the secret prefix method, $h(N_a, N_b, K_{ab})$ for the secret suffix method, and $h(K_{ab}, N_a, N_b, K_{ab})$ for the envelope method.

Returning to the 2PAP, A provides B with a nonce N_a in step (1), and B returns another nonce N_b together with $\langle N_a, N_b, B \rangle K_{ba}$ to A in step (2). A can now use K_{ba}

to verify the MAC, and to authenticate B accordingly. If B is considered as being authentic, A provides B with $\langle N_a, N_b \rangle K_{ab}$, which is another MAC computed from the concatentaion of N_a and N_b with the secret key K_{ab}, in step (3). B can now use K_{ab} to verify the MAC, and to authenticate A accordingly.

The developers of the original 2PAP have shown that the protocol is indeed resistant against interleaving attacks, and all KK protocols inherit this property. As a matter of fact, the design methodology for the key distribution protocols that follow is the reduction to 2PAP. In other words, if a protocol can be shown to be equivalent to 2PAP, then one can argue that it inherits some of the basic properties of this protocol, such as its resistance against interleaving attacks.

3.2.2   Two-Party Key Distribution

The objective of a two-party key distribution protocol (2PKDP) is to allow a principal A who already shares a secret key K_a with a key distribution center (KDC) to be provided with a new secret key K_a^{new}. The assumptions that have driven the design of the KK key distribution protocols are as follows:

- A key is always generated by just one party.
- A key being distributed must be a random and unpredictable quantity. If A and B engage in a key distribution protocol and A generates the key, then neither B nor any other party must be able to predict the key.
- Keys are never reused. Consequently, if a key is generated and distributed once, it will never be used again.

These assumptions have led to the important observation that a new key is conceptually similar to a nonce. In fact, the only difference between a new key that is distributed in a 2PKDP execution and a nonce that is used in a 2PAP execution is that the nonce is generally communicated in the clear, whereas the key must be communicated confidentially. In addition to that, the integrity and authenticity of the key may be protected, too. Consequently, the KK protocol family comprises two 2PKDPs: one that provides key confidentiality and one that additionally provides key integrity and authenticity.

Two-Party Key Distribution Protocol (2PKDP)

Drawing on the previous subsection, a simple 2PKDP can be derived from the basic 2PAP by simply replacing B with a KDC. The resulting 2PKDP can be formalized as follows:

$$
\begin{array}{rcl}
1 : \text{A} & \longrightarrow & \text{KDC} : N_a \\
2 : \text{KDC} & \longrightarrow & \text{A} \quad : N_k, \langle N_a, N_k, KDC \rangle K_a \oplus K_a^{new} \\
[\;\; 3 : \text{A} & \longrightarrow & \text{KDC} : \langle N_a, N_k \rangle K_a \;\;]
\end{array}
$$

Similar to 2PAP, A provides the KDC with a nonce N_a in step (1). The KDC randomly selects another nonce N_k and a new secret key K_a^{new} for A. The KDC then uses K_a to compute an MAC from both nonces and his or her own identifier, and adds the result bitwise modulo 2 to the new secret key K_a^{new}. In step (2), the KDC provides A with both N_k and $\langle N_a, N_k, KDC \rangle K_a \oplus K_a^{new}$. Note at this point that an eavesdropper who is able to grab the message can extract no information, unless he or she holds A's secret key K_a. A can now use K_a and N_k to compute $\langle N_a, N_k, KDC \rangle K_a$, and use this MAC to extract K_a^{new} from $\langle N_a, N_k, KDC \rangle K_a \oplus K_a^{new}$. Therefore, A has to add the MAC bitwise modulo 2 to $\langle N_a, N_k, KDC \rangle K_a \oplus K_a^{new}$, and the result should correspond to K_a^{new}. In step (3), A may provide the KDC with another MAC that is computed from both nonces N_a and N_k with K_a. Note that unlike the 2PAP, step (3) is generally not required in the 2PKDP. As a matter of fact, this optional step is usually not used since it would require the KDC to keep state between steps (2) and (3).

Two-Party Authenticated Key Distribution Protocol (2PAKDP)

The 2PKDP as described before is secure in the sense of key confidentiality, meaning that no one other than the KDC and A can obtain K_a^{new} [10]. However, the protocol is not secure in the sense of key integrity and authenticity. In other words, an intruder can modify the message that the KDC returns to A in step (2) of a 2PKDP execution, and cause A to extract a key that was not originally selected by the KDC. The problem is caused by the fact that A after receiving N_k and $\langle N_a, N_k, KDC \rangle K_a \oplus K_a^{new}$ in step (2) has no possibility to find out whether the received message is integer and authentic. As a matter of fact, the KDC may not be available and the entire message that is sent may have been concocted by an intruder.

At this point, however, it should be noted that this vulnerability is not a protocol failure, because the intruder cannot change the key to a known value. All the intruder can do is offset the key, meaning that he can fool A to accept $K_a^{new} \oplus X$ instead of K_a^{new}, with X being a value randomly chosen by the intruder. Nevertheless, the following two-party authenticated key distribution protocol (2PAKDP) has been designed to overcome this vulnerability:

$$
\begin{aligned}
1 &: A & \longrightarrow & \quad KDC : N_a \\
2 &: KDC & \longrightarrow & \quad A \quad : MAC(A), \{MAC(A)\}K_a \oplus N_k \\
[\ 3 &: A & \longrightarrow & \quad KDC : \langle N_a, N_k \rangle K_a \ ]
\end{aligned}
$$

Note that the format of the 2PAKDP is very similar to the 2PKDP. Again, A provides the KDC with a nonce N_a in step (1), and the KDC returns a message that consists of two parts in step (2). If the term $MAC(A)$ is used to abbreviate $\langle N_a, N_k, KDC \rangle K_a$, then the two parts of the message can be written as $MAC(A)$ and $\{MAC(A)\}K_a \oplus N_k$. Note that K_a^{new} doesn't appear in either of the two parts. The reason for this is that in the 2PAKDP, N_k not only represents the nonce chosen by the KDC, but the new key for A as well. Remember that we have found no fundamental difference between a key distributed in a key distribution protocol, and a nonce used in an authentication protocol. The idea of using the same value for both of them has thus led to the current design of the 2PAKDP. The implication of using N_k as a new key is that N_k can no longer be transmitted in the clear. Instead, it is hidden inside the message that the KDC sends to A in step (2). Although this message resembles in many respects the corresponding 2PAP and 2PKDP messages, the distinctive feature of 2PAKDP is its braided structure.

Upon receiving $MAC(A)$ and $\{MAC(A)\}K_a \oplus N_k$ in step (2) of the 2PAKDP, A encrypts the first part of the message, namely $MAC(A)$, with the secret key K_a that he shares with the KDC. A then computes $\{MAC(A)\}K_a$ and uses this value to factor out N_k from the second part of the message, namely from $\{MAC(A)\}K_a \oplus N_k$. Finally, A uses K_a to recompute the MAC $\langle N_a, N_k, KDC \rangle K_a$, and to check whether the result matches $MAC(A)$ that was received from the KDC at first place.

Again similar to the 2PKDP, step (3) is optional in the 2PAKDP. In this additional protocol step, A may provide the KDC with an MAC that is computed from both nonces with his secret key K_a.

3.2.3   Three-Party Key Distribution

The general objective of a three-party key distribution protocol (3PKDP) is to have a KDC distribute a session key to a pair of principals, such as A and B. A secure 3PKDP must satisfy very much the same conditions as a secure 2PKDP with the added requirement that neither principal must be able to alter the key being distributed.

Since initially A and B have no shared secret key that they could use as session key, they must contact the KDC with which they each share a secret key. The KDC is then to provide A and B with tickets. In NetSP, a *ticket* refers to a message that is issued by a KDC and sent in a message of a 3PKDP. Note that this terminology slightly differs from Kerberos.

With regard to three-party key distribution, it is generally not necessary for both principals to contact the KDC. Depending on whether A or B initially contacts the KDC, and whether a pull or push model is used, several 3PKDPs have been designed to meet the requirements of specific scenarios. Let's have a look at the A-B-KDC pull scenario and the KDC-A-B push scenario first. However, we can note at this point that all 3PKDPs combine in one way or another 2PAP executions and 2PKDP (or 2PAKDP) executions.

A-B-KDC Pull Scenario

In the *A-B-KDC pull scenario* it is assumed that A is either unable, unauthorized, or unwilling to contact the KDC, and that B is to replace A accordingly. A 3PKDP for the A-B-KDC pull scenario can be designed by simply combining and interleaving two 2PAKDP executions (one between A and the KDC and one between B and the KDC) and one 2PAP execution (between A and B). The resulting 3PKDP can be formalized as follows:

$$
\begin{aligned}
1 : A \quad &\longrightarrow \quad B \quad : N_a \\
2 : B \quad &\longrightarrow \quad KDC : N_a, N_b, A \\
3 : KDC &\longrightarrow \quad B \quad : MAC(A), \{MAC(A)\}K_a \oplus K_{ab}, \\
: \quad\;\; &\qquad\qquad\quad\; : MAC(B), \{MAC(B)\}K_b \oplus K_{ab} \\
4 : B \quad &\longrightarrow \quad A \quad : MAC(A), \{MAC(A)\}K_a \oplus K_{ab}, \\
: \quad\;\; &\qquad\qquad\quad\; : N_b, \langle N_a, N_b, B \rangle K_{ab} \\
5 : A \quad &\longrightarrow \quad B \quad : \langle N_a, N_b \rangle K_{ab}, [\langle N_a, K_{ab} \rangle K_a] \\
6 : B \quad &\longrightarrow \quad KDC : [\langle N_a, K_{ab} \rangle K_a, \langle N_b, K_{ab} \rangle K_b]
\end{aligned}
$$

Again, A provides B with a nonce N_a in step (1). In step (2), B provides the KDC with N_a and another nonce N_b, as well as A's identifier. In step (3), the KDC returns two tickets that contain the new session key K_{ab} to B. The tickets follow the same format as in the 2PAKDP, so $MAC(A)$ abbreviates $\langle N_a, K_{ab}, B \rangle K_a$, and $MAC(B)$ abbreviates $\langle N_b, K_{ab}, A \rangle K_b$. Having received the tickets, B can extract K_{ab} from $MAC(B)$ and $\{MAC(B)\}K_b \oplus K_{ab}$, and verify its integrity and authenticity by recomputing $\langle N_b, K_{ab}, A \rangle K_b$, encrypting it with K_b, and checking the result against

$MAC(B)$. If everything looks fine, B accepts K_{ab} as being the new session key to be shared with A.

In step (4), B forwards the other ticket, which consists of the two parts $MAC(A)$ and $\{MAC(A)\}K_a \oplus K_{ab}$, to A. In addition to that, B also provides A with the nonce N_b and $\langle N_a, N_b, B \rangle K_{ab}$. Similar to B, A can now use his ticket to extract and verify the new session key K_{ab}. A can use this key to verify $\langle N_a, N_b, B \rangle K_{ab}$ that he has just received from B. If the MAC turns out to be valid, A provides B with $\langle N_a, N_b \rangle K_{ab}$ in step (5). Note that this message may optionally include a confirmation token $\langle N_a, K_{ab} \rangle K_a$ to complete the mutual authentication between A and the KDC. Obviously, B can now complete the 2PAP execution between A and B. In addition to that, B can also optionally compute a confirmation token $\langle N_b, K_{ab} \rangle K_b$, and forward it along with A's confirmation token to the KDC in step (6). Note that the purpose of the optional confirmation tokens in steps (5) and (6) is just to acknowledge to the KDC that both A and B have indeed received the session key K_{ab}, and that they have successfully authenticated one other.

KDC-A-B Push Scenario

In the *KDC-A-B push scenario* A contacts B before requesting the tickets from the KDC. The corresponding 3PKDP can be formalized as follows:

$$
\begin{array}{llll}
1: A & \longrightarrow & B & : N_a \\
2: B & \longrightarrow & A & : N_b, \langle N_a, N_b, B \rangle K_b \\
3: A & \longrightarrow & KDC & : N_a, N_b, B, \langle N_a, \eta_b, B \rangle K_a, A \\
4: KDC & \longrightarrow & A & : MAC(A), \{MAC(A)\}K_a \oplus K_{ab}, \\
 & & & : MAC(B), \{MAC(B)\}K_b \oplus K_{ab} \\
5: A & \longrightarrow & B & : MAC(B), \{MAC(B)\}K_b \oplus K_{ab}, [\langle N_a, N_b, B \rangle K_{ab}]
\end{array}
$$

Again, A provides B with a nonce N_a in step (1). But instead of contacting the KDC, B returns to A another nonce N_b together with a corresponding MAC $\langle N_a, N_b, B \rangle K_b$ in step (2). It is now up to A to request the tickets from the KDC. With respect to requesting these tickets, A considers the MAC provided by B as a new nonce $\eta_b = \langle N_a, N_b, B \rangle K_b$.

In step (3), A provides the KDC with N_a, N_b, B, $\langle N_a, \eta_b, B \rangle K_a$, and A, and in step (4), the KDC returns the requested tickets to A. The tickets basically consist of $MAC(A)$ and $\{MAC(A)\}K_a \oplus K_{ab}$ for A, and $MAC(B)$ and $\{MAC(B)\}K_b \oplus$

K_{ab} for B. Again, the term $MAC(A)$ abbreviates $\langle N_a, K_{ab}, B \rangle K_a$, and $MAC(B)$ abbreviates $\langle N_b, K_{ab}, A \rangle K_b$.

Note at this point that by issuing these tickets, the KDC confirms to both A and B that their respective authentication tokens are valid. Also note that if either of the tokens is corrupted, the KDC is, in general, not able to determine which one is faulty. In other words, the KDC can only confirm that either both tokens are valid or none. In case it is desirable to determine the corrupt token, the message that A sends to the KDC in step (3) must also include $\langle N_a, N_b, B \rangle K_b$.

A distinguishing feature of the forward-flow authentication provided in steps (3) and (4) is that a direct handshake between A and B is no longer required. In principle, it has already taken place indirectly through the KDC. In step (5), A provides B with $MAC(B), \{MAC(B)\}K_b \oplus K_{ab}$, as well as $\langle N_a, N_b, B \rangle K_{ab}$ if necessary. Note that the last expression is only required, if crosstalk between different protocol executions can't be safely omitted.

It is important to note that the 3PKDP for the KDC-A-B push scenario does not provide the same assurance as the 3PKDP for the A-B-KDC pull scenario. In the KDC-A-B push scenario, both principals are satisfied at the end of the protocol execution that their peer is authentic and currently online. In the A-B-KDC pull scenario, however, both principals gain an additional assurance that their peer is currently in possession of the new session key K_{ab}. This difference becomes moot when the two principals engage in subsequent communication secured with K_{ab}. However, since this is not always the case, the 3PKDP for the A-B-KDC pull scenario can be rearranged to provide a similar functionality for the KDC-A-B push scenario. The resulting protocol can then be formalized as follows:

$$
\begin{array}{llll}
1 : A & \longrightarrow & B & : N_a \\
2 : B & \longrightarrow & A & : N_b \\
3 : A & \longrightarrow & KDC & : N_a, N_b, B \\
4 : KDC & \longrightarrow & A & : MAC(A), \{MAC(A)\}K_a \oplus K_{ab}, \\
& & & : MAC(B), \{MAC(B)\}K_b \oplus K_{ab} \\
5 : A & \longrightarrow & B & : MAC(B), \{MAC(B)\}K_b \oplus K_{ab}, \\
& & & : \langle N_a, N_b, A \rangle K_{ab} \\
6 : B & \longrightarrow & A & : \langle N_a, N_b \rangle K_{ab}
\end{array}
$$

In this case, A and B exchange two nonces N_a and N_b in steps (1) and (2). In step (3), A contacts the KDC with N_a, N_b, and B's identifier, and in step (4), the KDC provides A with both tickets. Again, the tickets consist of $MAC(A)$

and $\{MAC(A)\}K_a \oplus K_{ab}$ for A, and $MAC(B)$ and $\{MAC(B)\}K_b \oplus K_{ab}$ for B. A can use his ticket to extract the session key K_{ab}. In step (5), A forwards B's ticket together with $\langle N_a, N_b, A\rangle K_{ab}$ to B. B can now use this ticket to extract and verify the session key K_{ab}, too. Afterwards, B can use K_{ab} to additionally verify $\langle N_a, N_b, A\rangle K_{ab}$, and to authenticate A accordingly. If B has to authenticate to A, too, B returns $\langle N_a, N_b\rangle K_{ab}$ to A in step (6).

There are situations that require A to get the tickets from the KDC before communicating with B. For being used in these situations, a timestamp-based version of the 3PKDP for the KDC-A-B push scenario can be used, too. This slightly modified protocol can be formalized as follows:

$$
\begin{array}{llll}
1 : A & \longrightarrow & KDC & : N_a, B \\
2 : KDC & \longrightarrow & A & : MAC(A), \{MAC(A)\}K_a \oplus K_{ab}, \\
\ : & & & : T, MAC(B), \{MAC(B)\}K_b \oplus K_{ab} \\
3 : A & \longrightarrow & B & : N_a, T, MAC(B), \{MAC(B)\}K_b \oplus K_{ab} \\
4 : B & \longrightarrow & A & : N_b, \langle N_a, N_b, B\rangle K_{ab} \\
5 : A & \longrightarrow & B & : \langle N_a, N_b\rangle K_{ab}
\end{array}
$$

Note that in this protocol description, $MAC(A)$ ($MAC(B)$) abbreviates $\langle T, K_{ab}, B\rangle K_a$ ($\langle T, K_{ab}, A\rangle K_b$), with T being a timestamp generated by the KDC. Also note that the protocol structure is quite similar to Kerberos, and that the timestamp-based version of the 3PKDP for the KDC-A-B push scenario also requires loosely synchronized clocks at least between B and the KDC.

In step (1), A provides the KDC with a nonce N_a and B's identifier. In step (2), the KDC returns a timestamp T and both tickets to A. Again, the tickets consist of $MAC(A)$ and $\{MAC(A)\}K_a \oplus K_{ab}$ for A, and $MAC(B)$ and $\{MAC(B)\}K_b \oplus K_{ab}$ for B. A can use the ticket to extract and verify the new session key K_{ab}. In step (3), A forwards N_a, T, $MAC(B)$, and $\{MAC(B)\}K_b \oplus K_{ab}$ to B. Equipped with a ticket, B can extract and verify the new session key K_{ab}, too. B then randomly selects another nonce N_b, and provides A with both N_b and $\langle N_a, N_b, B\rangle K_{ab}$ in step (4). If A has extracted the correct session key K_{ab}, A can now verify $\langle N_a, N_b, B\rangle K_{ab}$, and return $\langle N_a, N_b\rangle K_{ab}$ to B in step (5) accordingly.

The distinguishing feature of the timestamp-based version of the 3PKDP for the KDC-A-B push scenario is the lack of challenge from B to the KDC. Instead, the freshness of the KDC's ticket for B is established on the basis of a timestamp that is supplied by the KDC. The protocol is thus hybrid in the sense that authentication between A and the KDC, as well as between A and B is based on a challenge-response mechanism, whereas authentication between B and the KDC is based on the use of a timestamp.

If clock synchronization between A and B is available, the protocol can be simplified to resemble even more the Kerberos protocol. In this case, the 3PKDP can be formalized as follows:

$$
\begin{array}{llll}
1: & A & \longrightarrow & KDC : N_a, B \\
2: & KDC & \longrightarrow & A \quad : MAC(A), \{MAC(A)\}K_a \oplus K_{ab}, \\
 & : & & \quad : T, MAC(B), \{MAC(B)\}K_b \oplus K_{ab} \\
3: & A & \longrightarrow & B \quad : N_a, T, \langle N_a, T, A \rangle K_{ab}, MAC(B), \{MAC(B)\}K_b \oplus K_{ab} \\
4: & B & \longrightarrow & A \quad : \langle N_a, T \rangle K_{ab} \text{ or } N_b, \langle N_a, N_b \rangle K_{ab}
\end{array}
$$

In step (1), A provides the KDC with a nonce N_a and B's identifier. In step (2), the KDC returns a timestamp T and both tickets to A. A uses a ticket to extract and verify the new session key K_{ab}, then uses this key to compute $\langle N_a, T, A \rangle K_{ab}$, and provides B with this MAC together with $N_a, T, MAC(B)$, and $\{MAC(B)\}K_b \oplus K_{ab}$ in step (3). B can use this ticket to extract and verify K_{ab}, too. Similarly, B can use K_{ab} to verify $\langle N_a, T, A \rangle K_{ab}$, and to authenticate A accordingly. If mutual authentication is required, B returns either $\langle N_a, T \rangle K_{ab}$ or $N_b, \langle N_a, N_b \rangle K_{ab}$ to A in step (4). Note that in this 3PKDP, instead of waiting for B's challenge, A authenticates to B in step (3) by including $\langle N_a, T, A \rangle K_{ab}$. Step (4) can then be reduced to carry either $\langle N_a, T \rangle K_{ab}$ or $N_b, \langle N_a, N_b \rangle K_{ab}$, and step (5) can be omitted altogether.

3.2.4   Interdomain Key Distribution

In principle, all 3PKDPs can be extended to support interdomain key distribution. Remember that in the Kerberos model, it is up to the client to request all tickets that are needed to contact a server in a remote realm, and that this may put a lot of work on the client side. The Kerberos model is therefore reasonable in a local area environment. However, there exist environments in which it is a poor match, because it is either prohibitive in terms of costs or not applicable at all. Again, the objective of flexibility has driven the design of the KK interdomain key distribution protocols, and different protocols have thus been designed to be used in different environments.

Similar to the Kerberos model, it is assumed that interdomain keys already exist. In principle, an interdomain key refers to a key that is shared between the KDCs of different administration and authentication domains. If the two KDCs are KDC_1 and KDC_2, then the term K_{12} is used to refer to the interdomain key that is used by KDC_1 and KDC_2 for interdomain authentication and key distribution. In spite of the fact that the capital letter implies the use of secret key cryptography, there is, in general, no reason why public key cryptography could not be used for interdomain authentication and key distribution. As a matter of fact, the use of public key cryptography can be made visible only to the KDC involved and transparent to the principals. Besides its many advantages, the most obvious disadvantage of using public key cryptography is an increase in message length and packet size.

We first discuss interdomain key distribution without inter-KDC communication, and focus then on interdomain key distribution with inter-KDC communication.

Without Inter-KDC Communication

In the simplest case, it is assumed that the KDCs do not engage in interdomain communication. Note that in spite of its simplicity, this assumption is sometimes quite realistic, because a KDC is usually a highly protected security server and communication with the outside world may put it in undue exposure. Furthermore, interdomain communication is often less predictable and less reliable than intradomain communication. Thus, the burden on the KDC can be significantly reduced by disallowing inter-KDC communication at all.

If direct communication between KDCs is unavailable, the obvious solution is for one of the KDCs to issue both tickets, and for the other KDC to translate the appropriate ticket for its constituent principal. For example, the 3PKDP for the A-B-KDC pull scenario can be extended accordingly. If A (B) is registered with KDC_1 (KDC_2), and KDC_1 and KDC_2 share the interdomain key K_{12}, then the corresponding interdomain 3PKDP can be formalized as follows:

$$
\begin{array}{llll}
1:A & \longrightarrow & B & : N_a \\
2:B & \longrightarrow & KDC_2 & : N_a, N_b, A \\
3:KDC_2 & \longrightarrow & B & : MAC(12), \{MAC(12)\}K_{12} \oplus K_{ab}, \\
& & & : MAC(B), \{MAC(B)\}K_b \oplus K_{ab} \\
4:B & \longrightarrow & A & : MAC(12), \{MAC(12)\}K_{12} \oplus K_{ab}, \\
& & & : N_b, \langle N_a, N_b, B \rangle K_{ab} \\
5:A & \longrightarrow & KDC_1 & : B, N_a, MAC(12), \{MAC(12)\}K_{12} \oplus K_{ab} \\
6:KDC_1 & \longrightarrow & A & : MAC(A), \{MAC(A)\}K_a \oplus K_{ab} \\
7:A & \longrightarrow & B & : \langle N_a, N_b \rangle K_{ab}
\end{array}
$$

Again, the term $MAC(A)$ is used to abbreviate $\langle N_a, K_{ab}, B \rangle K_a$, and $MAC(B)$ is used to abbreviate $\langle N_b, K_{ab}, A \rangle K_b$. In addition to that, $MAC(12)$ is used to abbreviate $\langle N_a, K_{ab}, A, B \rangle K_{12}$.

Obviously, the first two steps of the protocol are the same as in the intradomain 3PKDP for the A-B-KDC pull scenario. A provides B with a nonce N_a in step (1), and B contacts his KDC, which is KDC_2, with N_a, N_b, and A's identifier in step (2). However, after having received this message, KDC_2 discovers that A is not registered in his domain. Consequently, KDC_2 extracts A's domain name from A's identifier, determines the corresponding KDC, which is KDC_1, and obtains the key K_{12} that he shares with this KDC. Similar to the Kerberos model, this key can be stored, for example, in a principal entry in KDC_2's database. It is then up to KDC_2 to generate a new session key K_{ab}, and to provide B with $MAC(12)$, $\{MAC(12)\}K_{12} \oplus K_{ab}$, $MAC(B)$, and $\{MAC(B)\}K_b \oplus K_{ab}$ in step (3). Note that this message includes a ticket for B, but does not include a ticket for A. The point is that KDC_2 does not know A's secret key K_a, and can't issue a ticket for A accordingly. Thus, instead of issuing a ticket for A, KDC_2 issues a ticket for A's KDC, which is KDC_1.

After having received the message sent in step (3), B can use his ticket to extract and verify the new session key K_{ab}. In step (4), B forwards $MAC(12)$ and $\{MAC(12)\}K_{12} \oplus K_{ab}$ together with an authentication token that consists of a nonce N_b and $\langle N_a, N_b, B \rangle K_{ab}$ to A. When A receives the forwarded ticket from B, A may either try to read it, or simply determine from B's name that B is registered in a different domain. In either case, the ticket is not readable, and in step (5), A forwards the ticket to KDC_1 for translation. KDC_1 verifies the ticket, extracts K_{ab}, and provides A with a ticket that is generated with A's secret key K_a in step (6). A can now extract and verify the new session key K_{ab} from that ticket. Again, the final step (7) is analogous to the intradomain 3PKDP.

The other 3PKDPs without inter-KDC communication between KDCs can be extended in a similar fashion. They are not further discussed in this book.

With Inter-KDC Communication

There are situations in which communication between KDCs is necessary. For example, one of the principals may have no connection to his KDC, or more generally, have no means of contacting a KDC be it his own or a foreign one. Communication between KDCs is also advantageous if KDCs have faster, cheaper, or even more secure communication facilities, so that KDCs can communicate among themselves more efficiently or more securely than with principals.

The actual protocol modifications needed to support inter-KDC communication are fairly trivial. In principle, every interdomain 3PKDP differs from its intradomain counterpart only insofar as two additional messages are transmitted between the KDCs involved. The additional protocol steps, however, are transparent to the principals, and the latter need not necessarily differentiate between an interdomain 3PKDP and its intradomain counterpart.

For example, the 3PKDP for the pull scenario can be modified as follows to additionally support inter-KDC communication:

$$
\begin{aligned}
1 : A &\longrightarrow B &&: N_a \\
2 : B &\longrightarrow KDC_2 &&: N_a, N_b, A \\
3 : KDC_2 &\longrightarrow KDC_1 &&: N_a, N_b, A, B \\
4 : KDC_1 &\longrightarrow KDC_2 &&: MAC(A), \{MAC(A)\}K_a \oplus K_{ab}, \\
 &&&: MAC(12), \{MAC(12)\}K_{12} \oplus K_{ab} \\
5 : KDC_2 &\longrightarrow B &&: MAC(A), \{MAC(A)\}K_a \oplus K_{ab}, \\
 &&&: MAC(B), \{MAC(B)\}K_b \oplus K_{ab} \\
6 : B &\longrightarrow A &&: MAC(A), \{MAC(A)\}K_a \oplus K_{ab}, \\
 &&&: \langle N_a, N_b, B \rangle K_{ab}, N_a, N_b, A \\
7 : A &\longrightarrow B &&: \langle N_a, N_b \rangle K_{ab}
\end{aligned}
$$

The abbreviations $MAC(A)$, $MAC(B)$, and $MAC(12)$ are analogous to the ones given the previous 3PKDP. In step (1), A provides B with a nonce N_a. In step (2), B provides his KDC, which is KDC_2, with N_a, another nonce N_b, and A's identifier. In step (3), KDC_2 provides A's KDC, which is KDC_1, with both the identifiers and the nonces of A and B. In step (4), KDC_1 randomly selects a new session key K_{ab}, and provides KDC_2 with tickets for A and KDC_2. KDC_2

uses K_{12} to extract and verify K_{ab} from his ticket. Equipped with this key, KDC_2 can generate a new ticket for B. In step (5), KDC_2 provides B with both tickets. B can extract and verify K_{ab} from his ticket, and forward A's ticket together with $\langle N_a, N_b, B \rangle K_{ab}$, N_a, N_b, and A to A in step (6). A can now extract and verify the new session key K_{ab}, too. Equipped with this key, A can verify $\langle N_a, N_b, B \rangle K_{ab}$, and authenticate B accordingly. If mutual authentication is required, A provides B with $\langle N_a, N_b \rangle K_{ab}$ in the final step (7). B can now verify $\langle N_a, N_b \rangle K_{ab}$, and authenticate A accordingly.

Note that in this 3PKDP, KDC_1 issues the tickets that actually contain the session key K_{ab}, whereas KDC_2 only translates the ticket for B. Alternatively, the roles of the two KDCs may be switched, and the corresponding steps (3) and (4) then look as follows:

$$3 : KDC_2 \longrightarrow KDC_1 : N_a, N_2, A, B, MAC(12), \{MAC(12)\}K_{12} \oplus K_{ab}$$
$$4 : KDC_1 \longrightarrow KDC_2 : MAC(A), \{MAC(A)\}K_a \oplus K_{ab}$$

In this case, KDC_2 provides KDC_1 in step (3) not only with N_a, N_b, A, and B, but with the ticket $MAC(12), \{MAC(12)\}K_{12} \oplus K_{ab}$ as well. KDC_1 then uses K_{12} to extract and verify K_{ab} from this ticket. In addition to that, KDC_1 can use K_{ab} to generate a new ticket for A. In step (4), KDC_1 simply returns the new ticket to KDC_2. Obviously, this protocol results in smaller messages, but also increases complexity on the side of KDC_2.

Similarly, the 3PKDP for the push scenario can be modified to support inter-KDC communication, too. The resulting 3PKDP can be formalized as follows:

$$
\begin{aligned}
1 : A &\longrightarrow B &&: N_a \\
2 : B &\longrightarrow A &&: N_a, N_b, \langle N_a, N_b, B \rangle K_b \\
3 : A &\longrightarrow KDC_1 &&: B, N_a, N_b, \eta_b, \langle N_a, \eta_b, A \rangle K_a \\
4 : KDC_1 &\longrightarrow KDC_2 &&: A, B, MAC(A), \{MAC(A)\}K_a \oplus K_{ab}, \\
& &&: MAC(12), \{MAC(12)\}K_{12} \oplus K_{ab}, N_a, N_b, \eta_b \\
5 : KDC_2 &\longrightarrow KDC_1 &&: MAC(A), \{MAC(A)\}K_a \oplus K_{ab}, \\
& &&: MAC(B), \{MAC(B)\}K_b \oplus K_{ab} \\
6 : KDC_1 &\longrightarrow A &&: MAC(A), \{MAC(A)\}K_a \oplus K_{ab}, \\
& &&: MAC(B), \{MAC(B)\}K_b \oplus K_{ab} \\
7 : A &\longrightarrow B &&: MAC(B), \{MAC(B)\}K_b \oplus K_{ab}, [\langle N_a, N_b \rangle K_{ab}]
\end{aligned}
$$

Remember that we have introduced the term η_b to abbreviate $\langle N_a, N_b, B \rangle K_b$. In step (1), A provides B with a nonce N_a, and in step (2), B returns N_a, another nonce N_b, and $\langle N_a, N_b, B \rangle K_b$ to A. It is now up to A to contact his KDC, which is KDC_1, and to provide him with B, N_a, N_b, η_b, and $\langle N_a, \eta_b, A \rangle K_a$ in step (3). In step (4), KDC_1 provides the KDC of B, which is KDC_2, with A, B, $MAC(A)$, $\{MAC(A)\}K_a \oplus K_{ab}$, $MAC(12)$, $\{MAC(12)\}K_{12} \oplus K_{ab}$, N_a, N_b, and η_b. KDC_2 translates the second ticket into a ticket for B, and provides KDC_1 with $MAC(A)$, $\{MAC(A)\}K_a \oplus K_{ab}$, $MAC(B)$, and $\{MAC(B)\}K_b \oplus K_{ab}$ in step (5). Obviously, KDC_1 now forwards the entire message to A in step (6), and A extracts and verifies the new session key K_{ab} from the first ticket accordingly. In step (7), A provides B with the other ticket, which B can use to extract and verify K_{ab}, too.

Last but not least, the timestamp-based 3PKDP for the push scenario can be modified as follows:

$$
\begin{array}{llll}
1: A & \longrightarrow & KDC_1 : & N_a, B \\
2: KDC_1 & \longrightarrow & KDC_2 : & A, B, MAC(A), \{MAC(A)\}K_a \oplus K_{ab}, \\
 & & : & T_1, MAC(12), \{MAC(12)\}K_{12} \oplus K_{ab} \\
3: KDC_2 & \longrightarrow & KDC_1 : & MAC(A), \{MAC(A)\}K_a \oplus K_{ab}, \\
 & & : & T_2, MAC(B), \{MAC(B)\}K_b \oplus K_{ab} \\
4: KDC_1 & \longrightarrow & A & : MAC(A), \{MAC(A)\}K_a \oplus K_{ab}, \\
 & & : & T_2, MAC(B), \{MAC(B)\}K_b \oplus K_{ab} \\
5: A & \longrightarrow & B & : N_a, T_2, MAC(B), \{MAC(B)\}K_b \oplus K_{ab} \\
6: B & \longrightarrow & A & : \langle N_a, N_b, B \rangle K_{ab}, N_b \\
7: A & \longrightarrow & B & : \langle N_a, N_b \rangle K_{ab}
\end{array}
$$

In this 3PKDP, we have two timestamps T_1 and T_2 selected by KDC_1 and KDC_2 respectively. In addition to that, $MAC(A)$ $(MAC(B))$ is used to abbreviate $\langle N_a, K_{ab}, B \rangle K_a$ $(\langle T_2, K_{ab}, A \rangle K_b)$, and $MAC(12)$ to abbreviate $\langle T_1, K_{ab}, A, B \rangle K_{12}$.

In step (1), A provides his KDC, which is KDC_1, with a nonce N_a and B's identifier. In step (2), KDC_1 contacts the KDC of B, which is KDC_2. The message that is transmitted at this point consists of A and B's identifiers, a timestamp T_1, as well as $MAC(A)$, $\{MAC(A)\}K_a \oplus K_{ab}$, $MAC(12)$, and $\{MAC(12)\}K_{12} \oplus K_{ab}$.

In step (3), KDC_2 provides KDC_1 with a timestamp T_2 and two tickets for A and B, and in step (4), KDC_1 forwards the entire message to A. It is now up to A to extract and verify the new session key K_{ab}, and to provide B with N_a, T_2, $MAC(B)$, and $\{MAC(B)\}K_b \oplus K_{ab}$ in step (5). It is now up to B to extract and verify K_{ab}, too, and to provide A with another nonce N_b and $\langle N_a, N_b, B \rangle K_{ab}$ in step (6). A can use N_b to verify the MAC, and to authenticate B accordingly. If authentication succeeds, A provides B with $\langle N_a, N_b \rangle K_{ab}$ in step (7). B can now verify this MAC and authenticate A accordingly.

In spite of the fact that it is fairly trivial to modify 3PKDPs to support inter-KDC communication, it should be considered with care that the main consequence of this convenience is the sacrifice of the stateless nature of the KDCs. Remember that all key distribution protocols discussed so far allow KDCs to operate without having to keep state. In other words, a KDC receives a request and replies to it, without having to wait for an external event or keep any state with respect to this request. A KDC never initiates communication; it only responds. All this keeps the design and operation of KDCs comparatively simple. Inter-KDC communication, however, changes the simple nature of a KDC since it is now required to initiate communication with other KDCs, wait for responses, and deliver the results to the requesting principals.

3.2.5   Single Sign-On

Ideally, a single sign-on protocol should be a two-party authentication and key distribution protocol between a user and a security server, such as an AS or a KDC. In this respect, it appears that one could think of adapting the 2PAKDP to this task, too. However, a human user U is usually armed with only a weak secret key K_u derived from a relatively short alphanumeric password or a numeric PIN, so the use of this key should be minimized.

A naive approach to adapt the 2PAKDP for a single sign-on protocol could be formalized as follows:

$$
\begin{array}{llll}
1: \text{U} & \longrightarrow & \text{KDC}: & N_u \\
2: \text{KDC} & \longrightarrow & \text{U} & : MAC(U), \{MAC(U)\}K_u \oplus N_k
\end{array}
$$

In this protocol description, $MAC(U)$ is used to abbreviate $\langle N_u, N_k, KDC \rangle K_u$, with N_k representing both a nonce chosen by the KDC and the new key that is distributed to U. The protocol is quite simple: in step (1), U provides the KDC with a nonce N_u, and in step (2), the KDC returns $MAC(U)$ and $\{MAC(U)\}K_u \oplus N_k$. Note that U can use this message to extract N_k, and to verify the integrity and authenticity of the distributed key accordingly. Also note that, in general, step (3) from the 2PAKDP is not needed in the single sign-on protocol.

The reason for us to refer to this single sign-on protocol as a naive approach is due to the fact that an attacker can send a random nonce in step (1), and receive a corresponding response that is valid from the KDC in step (2). In general, the attacker is not able to factor out the session key directly, but can launch a password guessing attack. One possibility to deal with this problem is to require U to preauthenticate on the initial message that is sent to the KDC. The following timestamp-based single sign-on protocol meets this requirement:

$$1 : U \longrightarrow KDC : N_u, T, \langle N_u, T, U \rangle K_u$$
$$2 : KDC \longrightarrow U \quad : MAC(U), \{MAC(U)\} K_u \oplus N_k$$

In step (1), U provides the KDC with a nonce N_u, a timestamp T, and $\langle N_u, T, U \rangle K_u$. Note that U can compute the MAC only if he knows the secret key K_u. Consequently, it is not feasible for an intruder to initiate a single sign-on protocol execution without knowing the user's password. Note that the main drawback of requiring timestamp-based authentication is that this calls for clock synchronization between U and the KDC. This drawback is softened a little because the clocks need only be loosely synchronized as single sign-on frequency, in general, is assumed to be relatively low. Also note that step (2) has not changed compared to the single sign-on protocol described previously.

However, it should be made clear that the second single sign-on protocol renders more difficult password guessing attacks, but does not prevent them. The point is that an attacker can still grab the message that is sent from the KDC to U in step (2), and launch an offline password guessing or dictionary attack.

3.3   DISCUSSION

In summary, the KK protocols can be used to provide authentication and key distribution services in different network environments, and the keys that are distributed can then be used to additionally provide data confidentiality and integrity services.

The KK protocols have been designed with the goal of providing a high degree of compactness and flexibility. This goal has been achieved, and the KK protocol's message compactness, flexibility, and exportability make them an attractive solution for securing existing applications and communication systems at any protocol layer, irrespective of network configuration or communication paradigm. As a matter of fact, the KK protocols and variations thereof are being discussed for mobile communications networks [11], and the Internet, too.

With regard to the Internet, IBM has proposed an architecture to provide network layer security. At the heart of this architecture are two protocols, namely the IP secure tunnel protocol (IPST) and the modular key management protocol (MKMP):

- The IPST follows the spirit of discussions in the Internet Protocol Security Protocol (IPSEC) working group (WG) of the Internet Engineering Task Force (IETF). To protect the integrity and authenticity of an IP datagram, an MAC is computed and appended as a datagram header. To protect the confidentiality of an IP datagram, IP encapsulation is used. Consequently, an IP datagram is encrypted and placed in another datagram before transmission. The receiver is assumed to hold the keys that are necessary to decrypt the datagram, and to verify the MAC accordingly.

- The MKMP refers to a (set of) protocol(s) for the management of cryptographic keys as required for the management of security associations in IPST. The protocols provide secure mechanisms for periodic refreshment of keys and derivation of working keys as required for the cryptographic functions used with security associations.

The MKMP advocates a hierarchical approach. In particular, it assumes that two IPST entities A and B already share a long-term master key K_{AB}, and that they can use this key to negotiate short-term session keys K_{ab} if necessary. Note that the corresponding session key negotiation protocol, in principle, addresses a very similar problem as 2PKDP and 2PAKDP in the KK protocol family. However, the MKMP was designed to be as simple and efficient as possible.

Let's assume that A and B share a long-term master key K_{AB} and a nonce N_b from a previous protocol execution. In this case, they can use the MKMP to negotiate a short-term session key K_{ab}. The basic MKMP protocol can be formalized as follows:

$$1 : A \longrightarrow B : N_a, \langle N_a, N_b \rangle K_{AB}$$
$$2 : B \longrightarrow A : N'_b, \langle N'_b, N_a \rangle K_{AB}$$

In step (1), A randomly selects a nonce N_a, uses K_{AB} to compute $\langle N_a, N_b \rangle K_{AB}$, and provides B with both N_a and $\langle N_a, N_b \rangle K_{AB}$. In step (2), B selects another nonce N'_b, uses K_{AB} to compute $\langle N'_b, N_a \rangle K_{AB}$, and provides A with both N'_b and $\langle N'_b, N_a \rangle K_{AB}$. A and B both replace N_b by N'_b to be used in the following protocol execution. They now use a pseudorandom function f to derive the short-term session key $K_{ab} = f_{AB}(N'_b, N_a)$. Note that the function f is keyed with the long-term master key K_{AB}. This is necessary, because both arguments of the function, namely N_a and N'_b, are transmitted in the clear in steps (1) and (2) of the MKMP.

IBM has implemented the IPST and the MKMP [12]. It is selling the implementation as part of NetSP SNG, which is IBM's firewall product. In addition to that, IBM has proposed the MKMP to the IETF IPSEC WG for possible inclusion as part of a corresponding Internet standard. However, the proposal has been rejected in favour of other protocols, such as the Simple Key-Management for Internet Protocols (SKIP) or the Photuris[3] Key Management Protocol. More recently, IBM has has gathered up the MKMP proposal in favor of an enhanced version of the Photuris protocol named Photuris Plus or SKEME (Secure Key Exchange Mechanism) [13].

Eventually, the need arises to interconnect heterogeneous administration domains that use different authentication and key distribution systems. Designing mechanisms to interconnect heterogeneous domains is a challenging task, and if the heterogeneity also affects the security, the interconnection problem is even harder. In a sense, building a gateway that translates cryptographic tokens for security protocols safely is a contradiction per se in that the gateway must of necessity be involved in the translation of secure end-to-end flows, which makes these less secure. A first proposal of a possible interconnection model for Kerberos and NetSP was presented in [14]. Ongoing and future work has to refine and generalize this model.

Finally, it should be mentioned that IBM is shipping NetSP V1.2 with the commercial data masking facility (CDMF) built in as a standard secret key cryptosystem to provide data confidentiality services. In principle, the CDMF is a DES variant with a reduced key length of 40 bits [15]. Consequently, the use of the CDMF in NetSP represents a compromise between security and exportability. Equipped with CDMF, NetSP provides at least some confidentiality service. Not equipped with CDMF, NetSP would either offer confidentiality services but would not be exportable from the United States, or it would offer no confidentiality service and would be exportable from the United States accordingly. In this respect, the decision of IBM to dispense with using strong cryptography for encryption is more than understandable. However, the fact that NetSP is based on CDMF should be considered with care from the user's point of view.

REFERENCES

[1]   F.B. Cohen, "A Cryptographic Checksum for Integrity Protection," *Computers & Security*,

---

[3]"Photuris" is the latin name for the firefly, and "Firefly" is in turn the name for a classified key exchange protocol designed by the NSA for the STU-III secure telephone.

Vol. 6, 1987, pp. 505 – 510.

[2] L. Gong, "Using One-Way Functions for Authentication," *ACM Computer Communication Review*, Vol. 19, 1989, pp. 8 – 11.

[3] G. Tsudik, "Message Authentication with One-Way Hash Functions," *ACM Computer Communication Review*, Vol. 22, 1992, pp. 29 – 38.

[4] B. Kaliski, and M. Robshaw, "Message Authentication wirh MD5," *RSA Laboraties' CryptoBytes*, Vol. 1, 1995, pp. 5 – 8.

[5] B. Preneel, and P.C. van Oorschot, "MDx-MAC and Building Fast MACs from Hash Functions," *Advances in Cryptology — CRYPTO '95.* Springer-Verlag, 1995.

[6] R. Bird, I. Gopal, A. Herzberg, P.A. Janson, S. Kutten, R. Molva, and M. Yung, "Systematic Design of Two-Party Authentication Protocols," in J. Feigenbaum, editor, *Advances in Cryptology — CRYPTO '91*, Springer-Verlag, 1992, pp. 44 – 61.

[7] R. Bird, I. Gopal, A. Herzberg, P.A. Janson, S. Kutten, R. Molva, and M. Yung, "Systematic Design of a Family of Attack-Resistent Authentication Protocols," *IEEE Journal on Selected Areas in Communications*, Vol. 11, June 1993, pp. 679 – 693.

[8] R. Bird, I. Gopal, A. Herzberg, P.A. Janson, S. Kutten, R. Molva, and M. Yung, "The KryptoKnight Family of Light-Weight Protocols for Authentication and Key Distribution," *IEEE/ACM Transactions on Networking*, Vol. 3, February 1995, pp. 31 – 41.

[9] R. Molva, G. Tsudik, E. Van Herreweghen, and S. Zatti, "KryptoKnight Authentication and Key Distribution System," in Y. Deswarte, G. Eizenberg, and J.J. Quisquater, editors, *ESORICS '92 — European Symposium on Research in Computer Security*, Springer-Verlag, November 1992, pp. 155 – 174.

[10] G. Tsudik, and E. van Herreweghen, "On Simple and Secure Key Distribution," *in Proceedings of the 1st ACM Conference on Communications and Computing Security*, November 1993, pp. 49 – 57.

[11] R. Molva, D. Samfat, and G. Tsudik, "Authentication of Mobile Users," *IEEE Network*, Vol. 8, 1994, pp. 26 – 34.

[12] P.C. Cheng, J.A. Garay, A. Herzberg, and H. Krawczyk, "Design and Implementation of Modular Key Management Protocol and IP Secure Tunnel on AIX," *in Proceedings of the USENIX UNIX Security V Symposium*, USENIX Association, Berkeley, CA, 1995.

[13] H. Krawczyk, "SKEME: A Versatile Secure Key Exchange Mechanism for Internet," *in Proceedings of the Internet Society Symposium on Network and Distributed System Security*, February 1996.

[14] F. Piessens, B. De Decker, and P. Janson, "Interconnecting Domains with Heterogeneous Key Distribution and Authentication Protocols," *in Proceedings of the IEEE Symposium on Security and Privacy*, IEEE Computer Society Press, Los Alamitos, CA, 1993, pp. 66 – 79.

[15] D.B. Johnson, S.M. Matyas, A.V. Le, and J.D. Wilkins, "Design of the Commercial Data Masking Facility Data Privacy Algorithm," *in Proceedings of the 1st ACM Conference on Communications and Computing Security*, November 1993.

Chapter 4

SPX

In this chapter, we focus on the authentication and key distribution system SPX that was designed and prototyped by DEC. In Section 4.1, we summarize the development of the system, and in Section 4.2 we overview its architecture. In Sections 4.3 and 4.4 we describe and further discuss the cryptographic protocols that the system implements.

4.1 DEVELOPMENT

In the late 1980s, the Digital Equipment Corporation (DEC) proposed a distributed system security architecture (DSSA) that focused on the question of how to provide security services in a distributed environment [1,2]. With regard to its use of cryptographic techniques, the DSSA followed a hybrid approach, meaning that it assigned the use of secret key cryptography to provide data origin authentication, confidentiality, and integrity services, and the use of public key cryptography to provide entity authentication services.

The DSSA's authentication service was named distributed authentication security service (DASS). The service was prototyped in an authentication and key distribution system named *Sphinx* [3], and Sphinx was later renamed *SPX* [4]. Note that SPX is still pronounced Sphinx, and that nobody has come up with an acronym expansion for SPX so far.

SPX uses DES as a secret key cryptosystem, and RSA as a public key cryptosystem. However, the system is designed in a way that an alternate encryption algorithm could substitute DES with no or little disruption to the original architecture. SPX is implemented in a UNIX computing and TCP/IP network environment. Consequently, it is (or should be) portable to a variety of system platforms [5,6].

In spite of the fact that SPX has attracted much attention throughout the network security community, the development of the system was aborted after having released version 2.4 in December 1992. Today, DEC is promoting both a proprietary implementation of Kerberos V4 and OSF DCE products to meet the security requirements of its clients. As we have addressed Kerberos in Chapter 2 and have a look at OSF DCE in Chapter 7, we can confidently use this chapter to describe and discuss SPX.

SPX is publicly and freely available, today. Both source code and documentation can be downloaded from crl.dec.com (192.58.206.2) in the directory pub/DEC/SPX[1] Similar to Kerberos, SPX uses cryptographic techniques that are subject to U.S. export controls, and again we defer the discussion of the implications of this fact to Section 8.5. In addition to that, SPX uses the RSA public key cryptosystem that is patented in the United States. Consequently, access to the SPX source code is granted only under the condition that the recipient agrees not to tamper with either the RSA or the corresponding certification authority algorithms. The recipient also has to agree not to use the RSA implementation beyond its intended use within the SPX software package.

In January 1993, SPX was proposed as an experimental protocol to secure the telnet service in RFC 1412 [7]. In September 1993, a revised version of DEC DASS was proposed in RFC 1507 [8]. Note that unlike RFC 1510, which specifies Kerberos V5, RFC 1507 is not intended to specify an Internet standards track protocol, but to rather define an experimental protocol for the Internet community.

More recently, a simplified version of DEC DASS was proposed as simple public-key GSS-API mechanisms (SPKM) in a corresponding Internet-Draft. This work is still in progress and mainly driven by Bell-Northern Research.

---

[1]Note that DEC's gatekeeper FTP server distributes an older version of SPX, namely a beta version of SPX V2.0 that was released in February 1991.

4.2 ARCHITECTURAL OVERVIEW

SPX distinguishes between two classes of principals, namely human users and servers. Both can act as claimants and verifiers: If a principal acts as a *claimant*, he or she seeks to be recognized as authentic by a verifier, whereas as a *verifier*, a principal seeks to authenticate a claimant. Typically, human users act as claimants and servers act as verifiers.

In general, users are made accountable and ultimately responsible for what processes do on their behalf in computer networks and distributed systems. Processes are considered as representatives of users and must be authorized accordingly. The representation of a user in a process is coupled with a set of credentials, and these credentials include both the user's identity and a cryptographic key that is used for authentication. In principle, any process that can show that it knows this key may be taken as acting on the user's behalf. If a user process spawns another process on another host (e.g., by doing a remote login), credentials may be needed on the remote host, too. It may also be necessary to permit the remote process to do subsequent remote accesses on the user's behalf. In SPX, this kind of representation transfer is called *delegation*.

Depending on whether a principal is acting as a claimant or verifier, SPX uses different credentials:

- *Claimant credentials* are valid only for a relatively short period of time (the default value is eight hours). Claimant credentials are typically generated and installed when a user principal logs into a client workstation. They consist of

  - A short-term delegation private key;

  - A corresponding ticket.

  In principle, the ticket is just a certificate for the short-term delegation public key, digitally signed with the long-term private key of the principal. The aim of using short-term delegation keys is to minimize the potential for exposure of long-term private keys in untrusted environments as well as to limit the potential damage if a key actually gets compromised.

- *Verifier credentials* are typically generated and installed for server principals, and they directly include the corresponding long-term private keys. In general, verifier credentials are valid for a potentially long period of time.

It has been mentioned in the introduction that the use of public key cryptography, in general, requires an existant and fully operable certification hierarchy, and that this certification hierarchy is ideally coupled with a directory service and a corresponding naming scheme. When SPX was designed, it was assumed that a public key certification hierarchy would become available and widely deployed within the Internet community (e.g., for the evolving standards such as privacy enhanced mail (PEM) (Kent, 1993)).

With the exception of the syntactical representation of names, which is tied to ITU-T recommendation X.500, DEC DASS was designed to be independent of the particular underlying naming or directory service. While the intention is that certificates be stored in an X.500 service in the fields architecturally reserved for this purpose in the recommendation, the specification of DASS actually allows for the possibility of different forms of certificate stores. As a matter of fact, SPX implements its own certificate distribution service because its designers did not want to introduce a dependency on an X.500 directory service.

In SPX, X.509 public key certificates are created by a trusted and highly secure certification authority (CA). To reduce the impact of limited availability, the CA generates certificates that are stored in and distributed by online certificate distribution centers (CDCs). The CDCs needn't be trusted, and they can even be replicated for higher availability. In principle, a CDC represents a repository for public key certificates and other authentication information for principals. It is managed by an administrator who can add, update, and delete user and server certificate entries at will. In fact, a CDC simulates many of the characteristics of a directory service, and its use can be seen as an interim solution until an X.500 directory service becomes available and widely deployed.

Certificates are long lived and may get compromised during their lifetime. In order to have a possibility to securely revoke certificates that are compromised, SPX assumes certificates to be obtained from CDC replicas only. That is, a principal accepts a certificate only if both the CA and a CDC endorse it.

The CDC is accessed either during the login process, when creating claimant credentials for a user principal, or during the installation process, when creating verifier credentials for a server principal. In either case, the CDC provides the principal's encrypted private key and trusted authorities. The other time the CDC is accessed is when creating and verifying authentication tokens during a SPX authentication exchange. At these times the CDC provides certificates to be used in obtaining trusted copies of public key certificates for principals. The cryptographic protocols that SPX uses in either case will be described in the subsequent section. However, we want to mention at this point that if a CDC gets compromised, this may result in an interruption of certificate revocation or in a denial of service for principals, but would not allow an intruder to subvert the authentication scheme.

In addition to the CDCs, SPX uses a login enrollment agent facility (LEAF) to provide principals with encrypted copies of their long-term private keys, and to allow them to enroll themselves in the CDC. Similar to the CDCs, the LEAF was designed in a way that if it gets compromised, this may result in an exposure of the encrypted secret keys to password guessing attacks, but would not allow an intruder to subvert the authentication scheme.

SPX supports multiple trust relationships between principals and CAs. In a particular instance of authentication, the claimant and verifier need not necessarily trust the same CAs, nor does either need to trust all CAs. If a principal trusts a particular CA, this CA is called a trusted authority (TA) for this principal. The TAs of a principal thus correspond to the set of all CAs that the principal trusts. In principle, the TAs determine an authentication domain for the principal, with the authentication domain representing the subset of all principals capable of being authenticated.

In SPX, TAs are instantiated as a set of unique CA identifiers and corresponding public keys. They are installed along with the principal's credentials during the initialization process. SPX requires principals to have at least one TA, and if this is for the principal's immediate superior, such as his CA, the SPX also includes this CA's TAs. The current SPX implementation also includes the next level up, if the superior CA has a suitable TA certificate, but stops afterwards. However, SPX provides a utility for users to generate TA certificates.

In order to optimize certification paths, SPX permits a distinguished class of trusted CAs to authenticate other CAs. Consequently, a *cross certifying CA* is a CA that is trusted to issue certificates for arbitrary principals and CAs over which it may not have immediate jurisdiction. The current implementation of SPX supports cross certificates for CAs only within organizations and organizational units.

When verifying a certificate, SPX uses the principal's most explicit TA that applies to the certificate issuer name. In the simplest case, the principal would already know the public key of the issuer, and would use this key to verify the signature. The principal may also have a TA for a superior entry, in which case one would accept a path of certificates leading down from the TA to the subject certificate in question, as long as the issuer and subject names in intermediate certificates maintain the proper hierarchical relationship. If a signature can't be verified in one way or another, the certificate is rejected.

SPX principals use *authentication tokens* to authenticate each other. Like a Kerberos ticket, a SPX authentication token securely transfers a DES session key.

But unlike a Kerberos ticket, this session key is neither generated by a trusted third party nor is it encrypted with the receiver's secret key. In SPX, an authentication token is generated by the claimant and encrypted with the public key of the verifier. Therefore, principals need to know each other's public keys, and these keys are obtained from corresponding certificates that are received from the CDC. Principals who have successfully authenticated each other can use data origin, data confidentiality, and integrity services on a per-message basis by using the DES session key.

From the user's point of view, Kerberos and SPX provide a similar functionality, and the user interfaces are thus comparable. Table 4.1 summarizes the SPX user commands. Note that the system comes along with versions of the Berkeley r-tools that have been modified to incorporate SPX authentication (`fcp`, `flogin`, and `fsh`).

Table 4.1
SPX User Commands

SPX Command	Action
cdb_destroy	Destroy CDC database
cdb_edit	Edit CDC database
cdb_init	Initialize CDC database
cdb_list	List CDC database
createcertif	Generate a X.509 certificate
createkey	Generate a RSA key file
install_server	Install server credentials
spxdestroy	Destroy credentials
spxinit	Establish claimant credentials
spxlist	List contents of claimant credentials
fcp	Remote file copy (with SPX authentication)
flogin	Remote login (with SPX authentication)
fsh	Remote shell (with SPX authentication)

In order to incorporate security services into network applications, SPX provides a run-time library that supports a subset of the GSS-API (compare Appendix A). The GSS-API calls that are supported by SPX are summarized in Table 4.2. For example, acquiring credentials, using the `gss_acquire_cred()` call returns a credential handle to the application. Applications can acquire claimant, verifier, or both set of credentials. Once an application has acquired claimant credentials, it may initiate the establishment of a security context between the application and a peer application by calling `gss_init_sec_context()`. This call returns an authentication token, which is sent via the application protocol to the peer application. The peer application, which receives the authentication token, then calls `gss_accept_sec_context()` to accept the security context initiation. If the call is successful, the security context is established. If mutual authentication is required, the remote peer application returns an authentication token, too.

Table 4.2
SPX Supported GSS-API Calls

GSS-API Call	Action
gss_acquire_cred	Acquire credentials
gss_init_sec_context	Initiate outbound security context
gss_accept_sec_context	Accept inbound security context
gss_display_name	Translate name to printable form
gss_display_status	Translate status codes to printable form
gss_import_name	Convert printable name to normalized form
gss_release_buffer	Release storage
gss_release_name	”

4.3 CRYPTOGRAPHIC PROTOCOLS

In the following sections, we have a closer look at the SPX credentials initialization, authentication exchange, and enrollment protocols.

4.3.1 Credentials Initialization

If a user wants to delegate to his client workstation, he must have his long-term private key to install claimant credentials. In general, it is neither realistic to have users remember private keys nor to have them carry around smart cards or personal tokens with key files on them. It has already been mentioned previously that SPX provides a LEAF that allows users to get their encrypted private key. Note that the role of the LEAF as a login agent automatically diminishes as soon as smart cards or personal tokens become available and widely deployed.

It has also been mentioned previously that compromising the LEAF would not directly reveal private keys, but only expose them to password guessing attacks. The point is that the LEAF doesn't directly know a user's private key. Instead, the key is stored encrypted with DES and using a one-way hash derived from the user's password as key encryption key (KEK). In order to retrieve the private key, a principal must preauthenticate himself, meaning that the principal must provide evidence that he knows his password. To support this kind of preauthentication, the LEAF maintains an encrypted private key always together with another one-way hash of the user's password. This other one-way hash is generated using a different one-way hash function than the one used to form the KEK that encrypts the private key. The idea is to reveal the encrypted private key only if the one-way hash presented by the user matches the stored value.

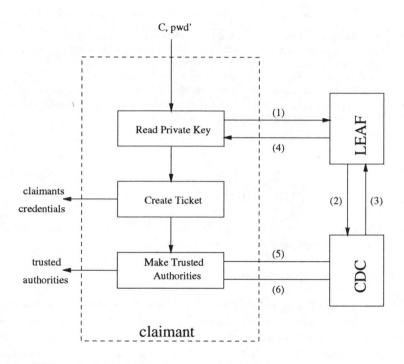

Figure 4.1   SPX credentials initialization protocol for a claimant.

The SPX credentials initialization protocol for a claimant is illustrated in Figure 4.1. The protocol consists of six steps that can be formalized as follows:

$$1 : C \quad\longrightarrow\quad \text{LEAF} : C, \{T, N_c, h_1(pwd')\}k_{LEAF}$$
$$2 : \text{LEAF} \quad\longrightarrow\quad \text{CDC} : C$$
$$3 : \text{CDC} \quad\longrightarrow\quad \text{LEAF} : \{\{k_C^{-1}\}h_2(pwd), h_1(pwd)\}K, \{K\}k_{LEAF}$$
$$4 : \text{LEAF} \quad\longrightarrow\quad C \quad : \{\{k_C^{-1}\}h_2(pwd)\}N_c$$
$$5 : C \quad\longrightarrow\quad \text{CDC} : C$$
$$6 : \text{CDC} \quad\longrightarrow\quad C \quad : C \ll (TA_C) \gg$$

The protocol starts with the assumption that the user who wants to initialize claimant credentials has already entered his identification C and password pwd'. Note that C is not only used to refer to the user principal's identification, but to the claimant credentials initialization process, too. This process, in general, is the login process. Also note that the apostrophe with pwd' is used to indicate that the user has yet entered a password, but that this password need not necessarily be the correct password pwd for C.

In step (1), C provides the LEAF with both identification and a message that is encrypted with the LEAF's long-term public key, which is k_{LEAF}. This key is assumed to be installed on the system that C is using e.g. in a publicly accessible configuration file. The encrypted message includes a timestamp T, a nonce N_c, and $h_1(pwd')$, which is a one-way hash of the password provided by C.

In step (2), the LEAF requests a CDC to be provided with the authentication information for C. This information basically consists of both $\{k_C^{-1}\}h_2(pwd)$ and $h_1(pwd)$.

In step (3), the CDC seals this information with a randomly selected DES key K, and provides the LEAF with both $\{\{k_C^{-1}\}h_2(pwd), h_1(pwd)\}K$ and $\{K\}k_{LEAF}$. Obviously, the LEAF can use his long-term private key k_{LEAF}^{-1} to decrypt $\{K\}k_{LEAF}$, and to extract the DES key K accordingly. The LEAF can then use K to decrypt $\{\{k_C^{-1}\}h_2(pwd), h_1(pwd)\}K$, and to extract $\{k_C^{-1}\}h_2(pwd)$ and $h_1(pwd)$ accordingly. If the one-way hash of the password from the CDC (which is $h_1(pwd)$) matches the value received from C (which is $h_1(pwd')$), the LEAF assumes C to know the correct password and to be authentic. Otherwise, an invalid password error message is returned and audited. Note that in this scheme, password guessing attacks require either knowledge of the LEAF's private key k_{LEAF}^{-1}, or contacting the LEAF for every single try. Consequently, SPX is assumed to be comparably resistant against password guessing attacks.

In step (4), the LEAF encrypts $\{k_C^{-1}\}h_2(pwd)$ with the nonce N_c that it has received in step (1), and provides C with $\{\{k_C^{-1}\}h_2(pwd)\}N_c$ accordingly. C can now use N_c and $h_2(pwd')$ to decrypt his long-term private key k_C^{-1}, and use this key to install claimant credentials. In order to do so, C randomly selects a short-term delegation public key pair (k_c, k_c^{-1}) and generates a corresponding login ticket $Ticket_C = \{C, k_c, L\}k_C^{-1}$. $Ticket_C$ includes C's identifier, C's short-term delegation public key k_c, and a lifespan L for the ticket. In addition to that, the login ticket is digitally signed with C's long-term private key k_C^{-1}. From now on, C doesn't use his long-term private key anymore, but uses the short-term delegation key k_c^{-1} instead.

The last thing that C has to do during credentials initialization is to install certificates for trusted authorities. In step (5), C provides the CDC with his identifier, and in step (6), the CDC returns $C \ll (TA_C) \gg$, which is a list of certificates for C's trusted authorities. The certificates are issued by C and digitally signed with C's long-term private key k_C^{-1}. After having received $C \ll (TA_C) \gg$, C holds a public key for all of his TAs. C can use these keys to subsequently verify digital signatures that are generally provided by them.

The current implementation of SPX uses ordinary files to store credentials. Because standard UNIX file access controls are used to protect these files, all processes that are running under a given user identity, in principle, share the same credentials. SPX also provides a user command to destroy credentials. Normally, when a user logs out, he would like to have his credentials deleted automatically. One way to achieve this is to put the corresponding SPX command in the .logout file. As general advice, it is recommended to enforce a security policy that doesn't allow expired credentials to remain on a system for more than about one day.

4.3.2 Authentication Exchange

The SPX authentication exchange is overviewed in Figure 4.2. The corresponding protocol can be formalized as follows (compare the message flows as illustrated in Figure 4.3):

$$
\begin{array}{llll}
1: C & \longrightarrow & CDC: V \\
2: CDC & \longrightarrow & C & : \langle TA_C, V, L_V, k_V \rangle k_{TA_C}^{-1} \\
3: C & \longrightarrow & V & : C, Ticket_C, \{K\}k_V, \{k_c^{-1}\}K \mid \{K\}k_c^{-1}, Auth_K \\
4: V & \longrightarrow & CDC: C \\
5: CDC & \longrightarrow & V & : \langle TA_V, C, L_C, k_C \rangle k_{TA_V}^{-1} \\
[\; 6: V & \longrightarrow & C & : Auth'_K \;]
\end{array}
$$

In step (1), the claimant C provides the CDC with the identifier of the verifier V he wants to authenticate to, and in step (2), the CDC provides C with a corresponding certificate $\langle TA_C, V, L_V, k_V \rangle k_{TA_C}^{-1}$. Note that TA_C is a trusted authority for C,

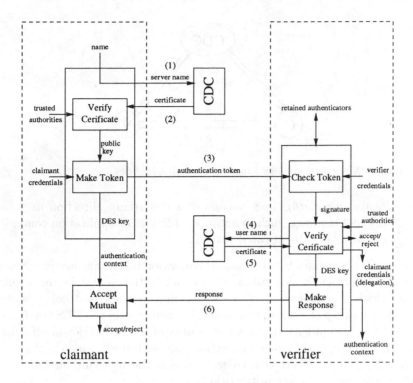

Figure 4.2   SPX authentication exchange overview.

and that C holds a public key that can be used to verify the digital signature that is appended to $\langle TA_C, V, L_V, k_V \rangle k_{TA_C}^{-1}$ accordingly. If the digital signature is valid, C extracts V's public key k_V from the certificate. In addition to that, C randomly selects a DES session key K, and uses this key to generate an authentication token. The authentication token consists of

- C;

- $Ticket_C = \{C, k_c, L\}k_C^{-1}$;

- $\{K\}k_V$;

- $\{k_c^{-1}\}K$, if delegation is required, or $\{K\}k_c^{-1}$ otherwise;

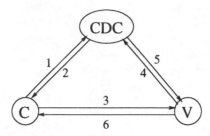

Figure 4.3   SPX authentication exchange protocol message flows.

- an authenticator $Auth_K$ that consists of a timestamp, direction flag, and optional channel bindings, such as network addresses or application context information. $Auth_K$ is authenticated with K.

In step (3), C provides V with the authentication token that has just generated. Note that the authentication token, in general, is transferred in the application protocol, which is independent of the underlying network protocols. V uses his credentials to unwrap the token, and to decrypt and recover the DES key K. V then uses K and the current time to check the validity of the authenticator. If delegation is required, V decrypts the delegation private key with the K, and checks it against the public key in the ticket. Otherwise, V checks the signature on the encrypted DES key using the public key in the ticket.

At this point, V has verified the validity of the authentication token, but still has to verify its authenticity. In step (4), V provides the CDC with C's claimed identity, and in step (5), the CDC returns $\langle TA_V, C, L_C, k_C \rangle k_{TA_V}^{-1}$. Note that this certificate is analogous to the certificate that was returned to C in step (2). Consequently, V can use the public key of TA_V to verify the digital signature that is appended to the certificate and extract k_C accordingly. Equipped with this key, V can then verify the digital signature that is associated with $Ticket_C$. If the signature is valid, V assumes C to be authentic. If delegation is required, there is an additional step in installing claimant credentials by using the ticket and the delegation private key.

If mutual authentication is required, V returns another authenticator $Auth'_K$ to C in step (6). In either case, C and V now share the DES key K, which they can use to provide data origin authentication, data confidentiality, and data integrity services.

SPX detects replay attacks on authentication exchanges by using timestamps in authenticators combined with remembering previously accepted messages until they become obsolete. This approach was chosen instead of other techniques, such as challenge-response mechanisms, mainly because of the desire to authenticate individual datagrams without pre-established shared authentication state. Another reason was the desire to achieve compatibility with Kerberos.

4.3.3 Enrollment

In general, having to enroll a large population of principals into a CDC causes a lot of work, and allowing principals to enroll themselves reduces the administrative burden considerably. Consequently, SPX allows principals to enroll themselves, and to add authentication information to the CDC so that they become generally available. The authentication information of a principal A consists of

- A's certificates;

- A's encrypted long-term private key $\{k_A^{-1}\}h_2(pwd)$;

- A one-way hash $h_1(pwd)$ of the corresponding password (if A is a user).

Obviously, a prerequisite for principal A to enroll into a CDC is to already have a long-term public key pair (k_A, k_A^{-1}) with corresponding certificates. As shown in Table 4.1, SPX provides user commands to create both of them. However, it is generally anticipated that they already exist for other purposes.

In addition to A's long-term public key pair and corresponding certificates, A has also to create a TA certificate for every single CA that he trusts, and to choose a password *pwd* that is used to create both the encrypted private key $\{k_A^{-1}\}h_2(pwd)$ and the one-way hash $h_1(pwd)$.

For the enrollment process itself, A has to randomly select a DES key K, too. Equipped with this key, A generates an enrollment request that is sent to the LEAF. The request consists of

- $Ticket_A$;

- A's certificates and TA certificates;

- $\{h_1(pwd), \{k_A^{-1}\}h_2(pwd)\}K$;

- $\{K\}k_{LEAF}$;

- An authenticator $Auth_K$.

The LEAF decrypts $\{K\}k_{LEAF}$ with its private key k_{LEAF}^{-1}. Equipped with K, the LEAF can decrypt $\{h_1(pwd), \{k_A^{-1}\}h_2(pwd)\}K$, and extract $h_1(pwd)$ and $\{k_A^{-1}\}h_2(pwd)$ accordingly. In addition to that, the LEAF can also use K to verify the authenticator $Auth_K$. If everything looks fine, the LEAF enrolls A's authentication information in the CDC.

4.4 DISCUSSION

SPX is an intersting authentication and key distribution system mainly because it was historically the first system not only to follow a hybrid approach, but also to use the new and evolving standards ITU-T X.509 (ITU, 1987) and ISO 9594-8 (ISO/IEC, 1990). However, the use of public key cryptography could have led to a system that provides more functionality than SPX actually does. In particular, it could have led to a system that additionally provides non-repudiation services.

With regard to a possible deployment of SPX, it should be considered with care that the system has never been widely used outside DEC's own research labs, and that it hasn't been further developed since version 2.4. As a matter of fact, SPX is not officially supported by DEC anymore. All designers of DEC DASS, as well as all developers of SPX have left the company meanwhile. Even the mailing list that was used to discuss SPX related topics has ceased to exist. Given these facts, it is not likely that SPX will ever regain much attention in the future.

REFERENCES

[1] M. Gasser, A. Goldstein, C. Kaufman, and B. Lampson, "The Digital Distributed System Security Architecture," *in Proceedings of the 12th National Computer Security Conference*, 1989, pp. 305 – 319.

[2] J. Linn, "Practical Authentication for Distributed Computing," *in Proceedings of the IEEE Symposium on Security and Privacy*, IEEE Computer Society Press, Los Alamitos, CA, 1990.

[3] J. Tardo, K. Alagappan, and R. Pitkin, "Public-Key Based Authentication Using Internet Certificates," *in Proceedings of the USENIX UNIX Security II Symposium*, USENIX Association, Berkeley, CA, August 1990, pp. 121 – 123.

[4] J. Tardo and K. Alagappan, "SPX: Global Authentification Using Public Key Certificates," *in Proceedings of the IEEE Symposium on Security and Privacy*, IEEE Computer Society Press, Los Alamitos, CA, 1991, pp. 232 – 244.

[5] K. Alagappan, *SPX Installation*, Digital Equipment Corporation, February 1991.

[6]   K. Alagappan and J. Tardo, *SPX Guide — A Prototype Public Key Authentication Service*, Digital Equipment Corporation, February 1991.

[7]   K. Alagappan, "Telnet Authentication: SPX," Request for Comments 1412, January 1993.

[8]   C. Kaufman, "DASS — Distributed Authentication Security Service," Request for Comments 1507, September 1993.

Chapter 5

TESS

The Exponential Security System (TESS) is a toolbox set system of different but cooperating cryptographic mechanisms and functions based on the primitive of discrete exponentiation. The system is being developed at the European Institute for System Security (EISS) of the University of Karlsruhe in Germany. In this chapter, we focus on the use of TESS for authentication and key distribution. In Section 5.1, we summarize the development of the system, and in Section 5.2 we overview its architecture. In Sections 5.3 and 5.4 we then describe and further discuss the cryptographic protocols that TESS is based on.

5.1 DEVELOPMENT

Given a finite group G, the *discrete exponentiation* in G refers to the n-fold composition of an element $\alpha \in G$ with itself:

$$n \mapsto \alpha^n = \alpha \cdot \alpha \cdot \ldots \cdot \alpha$$

In this notation, the multiplication is used to refer to the composition, and α^0 is used to refer to the neutral element in G. Note that the inverse of the discrete exponentiation, namely the *discrete logarithm*, is generally hard to compute. For

101

example, given a large prime p and a primitive element α in G, it is easy to compute $y = \alpha^x$ for a $x \in G$, whereas it is hard to compute x, given y, α, and p.

For all practical purposes, the *discrete exponentiation* in a finite group G is therefore considered as a good candidate for providing a one-way function in the sense of public key cryptography. In addition to that, it is worth mentioning that the discrete exponentiation in contrast to the RSA one-way function doesn't have an intrinsic trapdoor that can eventually be deployed to break the system.

Historically, the first group proposed as a basis for a public key cryptosystem was the multiplicative group $\mathbb{Z}_p$ of integers modulo a prime number p that actually is the multiplicative group of a finite field $GF(p)$. The basic operation in this group is integer multiplication modulo p. Since this operation can be performed relatively efficiently, $\mathbb{Z}_p$ is still considered as good choice for a software implementation. However, other groups are considered as valuable alternatives to $\mathbb{Z}_p$, too. Examples are the multiplicative group of an extension field $GF(p)^n$, which can be constructed from polynomials over $GF(p)$, elliptic curve groups, and subgroups of the aforementioned groups.

There are several security primitives based on the discrete exponentiation. The most popular examples are

- The *Diffie-Hellman key exchange* (Diffie and Hellman, 1976);

- The *ElGamal signature scheme* (ElGamal, 1984; ElGamal, 1985), and its variation proposed by Agnew, Mullin, and Vanstone [1];

- The *Digital Signature Standard* (DSS) proposed by the U.S. National Institute of Standards and Technology (NIST) in Federal Information Processing Standard (FIPS) 186 (NIST, 1994);

- The zero-knowledge scheme proposed by Chaum, Evertse, and van de Graaf [2], as well as its variants proposed by Beth [3] and Schnorr [4].

The Diffie-Hellman key exchange uses the one-way property of the discrete exponentiation to allow two principals A and B to exchange a secret key using a public channel. Provided that A and B have both agreed on a large prime p and a primitive element $\alpha \in GF(p)$, A (B) can select a random number x_a (x_b), and publish $y_a = \alpha^{x_a} (\text{mod } p)$ ($y_b = \alpha^{x_b} (\text{mod } p)$). According to the terminology used in public key cryptography, x_a (x_b) refers to A's (B's) private key, and y_a (y_b) refers to A's (B's) public key.

If A and B provide each other with their public key y_a and y_b respectively, they can agree on a common session key $K = K_{ab} = K_{ba}$ as follows:

$$K_{ab} = y_b^{x_a} = \alpha^{x_b x_a} = \alpha^{x_a x_b} = y_a^{x_b} = K_{ba}(\text{mod } p)$$

As a reader of this book, you are assumed to be familiar with both the Diffie-Hellman key exchange and its vulnerability to "man-in-the-middle" attacks. Note that if an attacker C controls the communication channel used between A and B, he can send $y_c = \alpha^{x_c}(\text{mod } p)$ to B upon receiving y_a from A, and y_c to A upon receiving y_c from B. If both A and B accept the faked messages, C subsequently shares a key $K' = \alpha^{x_a x_c}(\text{mod } p)$ with A, and another key $K'' = \alpha^{x_b x_c}(\text{mod } p)$ with B. Obviously, C can use these keys to decrypt, read, and possibly modify and reencrypt any message that is sent from A to B and vice versa.

The underlying problem that enables man-in-the-middle attacks in the Diffie-Hellman key exchange is due to the fact that the authenticity of the public keys y_a and y_a is not assured. As a matter of fact, this problem has been known since the original publication of Diffie and Hellman, and several possibilities have been proposed to overcome it [5].

An interesting possibility was independently discovered by Günther [6], and Bauspiess and Knobloch [7]. The basic idea is to use self-certified public keys, and to have these keys certified by a trusted third party that acts as a certification authority (CA). According to [8], a *self-certified* public key is a key that can be computed from its holder's identification and some other public information. The notion of a self-certified public key is thus similar to Shamir's notion of an identity-based cryptosystem [9]. The point is that the use of self-certified public keys in a key exchange protocol provides its participants with an authentic session key.

The Günther-Bauspiess-Knobloch protocol was named *KATHY*, an acronym derived from "KeY exchange with embedded AuTHentication." Having defined the basic KATHY protocol, the European Institute for System Security (EISS[1]) of the University of Karlsruhe in Germany started to develop other protocols that use self-certified public keys, too [10,11]. The development effort led to The Exponential Security System (TESS), which today is a toolbox set system of different but cooperating cryptographic mechanisms and functions based on the primitive of discrete exponentiation [12-15].

5.2   ARCHITECTURAL OVERVIEW

In this section, we overview the architecture of TESS. In Section 5.2.1 we focus on the TESS toolboxes, and in Section 5.2.2 we describe two corresponding application packages.

[1]http://avalon.ira.uka.de/eiss/

5.2.1   Toolboxes

TESS basically consists of five toolboxes which are implemented in the programming language C (ANSI-C) [16].

- A *long integer arithmetic toolbox* that supports arithmetic with long integer operands up to a length of 4,096 bits. The toolbox provides both

  - A set of low-level functions, such as addition, subtraction, multiplication, division, squaring, comparison, and others;

  - A set of high-level functions, such as modular multiplication, modular exponentiation, modular inversion, and others.

  Some of these functions are also available in optimized assembler code to increase performance.

- A *cipher toolbox* that consists of two modules, one handling stream ciphers based on linear feedback shift registers, and the other handling block ciphers. With regard to the second module, DES, FEAL, and IDEA are currently supported in ECB (electronic code book) mode. However, a special "modes of operation" module can be used on the top of these block ciphers to support their use in the CBC (cipher block chaining), OFB (output feedback), and CFB (cipher feedback) mode, too.

- A *chipcard toolbox* that implements a three-layer protocol suite for communications with chipcards. The first layer consists of a system-dependent module handling communications between a host system and a chipcard reader over a standard serial line. The current implementation supports the MS-DOS, Apple Macintosh, and UNIX operating systems. The second layer is used to drive a chipcard reader over a serial interface, and the third layer implements the actual transport protocols. To be used together with the chipcard toolbox, the EISS has developed a chipcard (ICECard) and a corresponding chipcard reader (ICEBox), too. The ICECard and ICEBox are currently being used in field trials.

- An *authentication toolbox* implements the KATHY protocols that are described in the next section. The toolbox provides three classes of application functions, namely

– Functions for starting an authentication and for terminating an encrypted session;

– Status functions that provide an application with various information about the state and the parameters of the authentication and the (authenticated) name of the communication partner;

– Some filter functions that may be used by an application to process all incoming and outgoing data.

In cooperation with the chipcard toolbox, the authentication toolbox can delegate calculations with a user's secret key to a chipcard.

• A *support toolbox* that contains functions to support a broad range of hardware platforms and operating systems.

Note that the programming language C was selected to increase the portability of the software. If a toolbox must be ported to a new platform, the C version usually compiles with no, or only minor, changes. Once the application is running, the base functions can be independently implemented and optimized in assembler code to gain speed.

5.2.2 Application Packages

TESS has been used to build two application packages so far, namely the SEcure Local Area Network Environment (SELANE) and the Exponential Electronic Signature (EES).

SELANE

The *SEcure Local Area Network Environment* (SELANE[2]) is a TESS application package that represents an authentication and key distribution system similar to the other systems described and discussed in this book. As a matter of fact, SELANE has been the main reason for us to dedicate this chapter to TESS.

As its name suggests, SELANE was initially conceived for a local area network environment. However, the system's name is somehow misleading, and there is

---

[2]The name SELANE is also intended to refer to Selene, an ancient goddess for the moon. Similar to Selene having the choice of selecting her lover Endymion, the user of SELANE is intended to have the choice of selecting any encryption algorithm.

nothing about SELANE or the cryptographic protocols that it implements that would restrict its use to the local environment. As a matter of fact, SELANE can be used to provide authentication, data confidentiality, and integrity services in any network or distributed environment.

SELANE has been implemented on the common workstation environments of MC680xx, Intel 80x86, VAX and SPARC processors under the UNIX, VMS, MS/DOS, and Apple Macintosh operating systems. The EISS is using SELANE to secure `telnet` access from both its local environment and the Internet on the institute's firewall host.

EES

The *Exponential Electronic Signature* (EES) system is another TESS application package that supports the generation and verification of ElGamal signatures.

The EES system was originally developed for electronic data interchange (EDI) and banking applications in 1989, when after an in-depth study of available signature schemes, the superiority of the exponential scheme became apparent. More recently, after the announcement of the DSS by the NIST, the role of the discrete exponentiation has regained proper recognition as being another security primitive besides RSA.

5.3   CRYPTOGRAPHIC PROTOCOLS

The use of TESS requires a trusted third party that serves as a certification authority (CA) or secure key issuing authority (SKIA). In the current implementation of TESS, the SKIA is a stand-alone program that runs on a personal computer without connection to the network. The SKIA' secret key is stored on a disk, which is encrypted using DES.

The general idea of TESS is to have a SKIA generate an identity descriptor m_A for every single user principal A, and to compute a corresponding ElGamal signature (r_A, s_A) for m_A. The pair (m_A, r_A) then represents the self-certified public key of A, whereas s_A represents the corresponding private key. In general, the connection between the two keys is the verification equation in the ElGamal signature scheme. In TESS, however, instead of verifying the ElGamal signature (r_A, s_A), the equation is used to calculate $r_A^{s_A}$ from public data without knowledge of the private key s_A.

In the following sections we describe the protocols that are used to initialize a SKIA, to register users, and to authenticate users to each other, as well as to generate and verify digital signatures.

5.3.1   SKIA Initialization

Provided that a large prime number p of at least 512 bit length and a primitive root $\alpha \in \mathrm{GF}(p)$ that may serve as a generator of $\mathrm{GF}(p)$ are known and the same for all SKIAs, one particular SKIA can be initialized by randomly selecting a private key $X \in \mathrm{GF}(p)$, and computing the corresponding public key

$$Y = \alpha^X (\mathrm{mod}\ p)$$

The triple (p, α, Y) represents the public key of the SKIA, whereas X represents the corresponding private key. Note that the one-way property of the discrete exponentiation suggests that the knowledge of Y doesn't reveal X. Since the triple (p, α, Y) is needed within the verification equation for the signatures generated by the SKIA, this triple is also an essential part of all user keys generated by this SKIA.

5.3.2   User Registration

With respect to the registration of user principal A, the SKIA generates an identity descriptor m_A that is precise enough to uniquely identify A. One way to achieve this is to describe A with his name, address, phone number, date of birth, and social security number, to convert this description into a bit- or byte-oriented representation, and to hash the result to a value that encodes a number in $\mathrm{GF}(p)$.

After this initial step, the SKIA chooses a random number $k_A \in \mathbb{Z}_{p-1}^* \backslash \{1\}$, computes $r_A = \alpha^{k_A}((\mathrm{mod}\ p))$, and solves the congruence

$$Xr_A + s_A k_A \equiv m_A (\mathrm{mod}\ p - 1)$$

for s_A. In order to do so, the SKIA has to compute

$$s_A = (m_A - Xr_A)k_A^{-1}(\mathrm{mod}\ p - 1)$$

The pair (r_A, s_A) then represents an ElGamal signature for m_A, with (m_A, r_A) being A's public key, and s_A being A's private key. Note that the SKIA may wish that A not know his secret key. This may be necessary because the user could otherwise reveal the secret key accidentally or intentionally. Especially if untrusted hardware or software is used in an environment that is not thoroughly protected, A's secret key may be spied out. For high-level security applications this is not acceptable, and A must be enabled to use his secret key without being able to read it. This apparent contradiction may be solved by using physically protected hardware devices, such as chipcards or personal tokens.

The value of k_A must be destroyed by the SKIA immediately after the registration of A. The problem is related to the fact that A could solve the congruence for the SKIAs private key X, if A knew both s_A and k_A. In addition to that, it should be made sure that the random number k_A is not used twice, and that s_A is not equal to zero.

We have already mentioned previously that Agnew, Mullin, and Vanstone have proposed a variation of the ElGamal signature scheme. This variation is commonly referred to as *AMV variation scheme* [1]. The basic idea of the AMV variation scheme is to interchange the roles of r and s in the ElGamal signature scheme. Instead of $m \equiv xr + ks \pmod{p-1}$, the signer thus solves the congruence $m \equiv xs + kr \pmod{p-1}$, and the signature (m, r, s) is verified by checking the equation $\alpha^m = y^s r^r$.

The main advantage of the AMV variation scheme over the standard ElGamal signature scheme is that in order to compute the signature by solving the congruence for s, the signer only needs to compute y^{-1} in $\mathbb{Z}^*_{p-1}$ once, instead of computing k^{-1} for every single signature.

In TESS, the use of the AMV variation scheme has led to a slightly modified KATHY protocol, namely the r^r-*KATHY protocol*. In this protocol, the SKIA solves the congruence

$$X s_A + r_A k_A \equiv m_A \pmod{p - 1}$$

for s_A, and therefore computes

$$s_A = (m_A - r_A k_A) X^{-1} \pmod{p - 1}$$

Note that this computation requires the inverse of X, which is the same for all users, whereas in the previous case k_A^{-1} was required, which is different for every user. Consequently, the use of the r^r-KATHY protocol allows X^{-1} to be precomputed once and for all users.

One point that should be considered with care is due to the fact that within the normal registration procedure for A, the SKIA gains knowledge about the actual value of A's secret key s_A. Consequently, the SKIA could use this key either to recompute any session key that A exchanges with another user B later on, or to fake signatures on A's behalf. The SKIA could even allow others to do so.

In order to avoid this comprising situation, a slight modification of the user registration procedure must be applied. In principle, A must have his identification string m_A digitally signed in a way that doesn't reveal the actual value of s_A to the SKIA. The basic concept that can be used for this purpose is the parameter hidden signature, a variant of the blind signature scheme introduced by Chaum [17]. In a parameter hidden ElGamal signature scheme, the SKIA knows m_A and r_A, but doesn't learn anything about s_A.

In TESS, a parameter hidden ElGamal signature is also referred to as a *testimonial*. In principle, the SKIA testifies that s_A belongs to A without knowing the actual value of s_A. The testimonial is generated as follows: A selects a random number $t_A \in \mathbb{Z}_{p-1}^*$ and computes $\beta = \alpha^{t_A} (\mathrm{mod}\ p)$. A then provides the SKIA with the value of β, and the SKIA uses β instead of α for all subsequent computational steps. In particular, the SKIA randomly selects $k_A \in \mathbb{Z}_{p-1}^*$ with $(k_A, p-1) = 1$, computes $r_A = \beta^{k_A} (\mathrm{mod}\ p)$, and solves the congruence

$$Xr_A + b_A k_A \equiv m_A(\mathrm{mod}\ p - 1)$$

for b_A, and provides A with the triple (m_A, r_A, b_A). Again, the pair (r_A, b_A) represents an ElGamal signature for m_A. In order to extract s_A from b_A, A has to compute $s_A = b_A t_A^{-1} (\mathrm{mod}\ p - 1)$. Note that without knowing t_A and t_A^{-1}, respectively, the SKIA is not able to learn anything about the actual value of s_A.

5.3.3   Authentication

If A and B are registered in the same administration domain, they both know the public key Y of their appropriate SKIA. Furthermore, if A has used the basic protocol for registration, he can use the following protocol to initiate a key exchange with embedded authentication with B:

$$
\begin{array}{lll}
1 : A & \longrightarrow & B : m_A, r_A \\
2 : B & \longrightarrow & A : v_a = r_A^{z_a}(\mathrm{mod}\ p)
\end{array}
$$

In step (1), A provides B with his public parameters m_A and r_A. B randomly selects a $z_a \in \mathbb{Z}_{p-1}^*$, computes $v_a = r_A^{z_a}(\mathrm{mod}\ p)$, and provides A with v_a in step (2). If A computes $K_a' = v_a^{s_A}(\mathrm{mod}\ p)$, and B computes $K_a'' = (\alpha^{m_A} Y^{-r_A})^{z_a}(\mathrm{mod}\ p)$, they in fact end up with the same session key $K_a = K_a' = K_a''$.

In order to show that K_a' and K_a'' are indeed the same key, we have to show that $v_A^{s_A} \equiv (r_A^{z_A})^{s_A} \equiv (r_A^{s_A})^{z_A}(\mathrm{mod}\ p)$ is the same as $(\alpha^{m_A} Y^{-r_A})^{z_A}(\mathrm{mod}\ p)$, or $r_A^{s_A}$ is the same as $\alpha^{m_A} Y^{-r_A}(\mathrm{mod}\ p)$ accordingly. On the one hand $r_A^{s_A} \equiv \alpha^{k_A s_A}(\mathrm{mod}\ p)$, and on the other hand

$$\alpha^{m_A}Y^{-r_A} \equiv \alpha^{Xr_A+s_Ak_A}Y^{-r_A}(\text{mod } p)$$
$$\equiv \alpha^{Xr_A}\alpha^{s_Ak_A}Y^{-r_A}(\text{mod } p)$$
$$\equiv \alpha^{Xr_A}\alpha^{s_Ak_A}\alpha^{-Xr_A}(\text{mod } p)$$
$$\equiv \alpha^{s_Ak_A}(\text{mod } p)$$

Note that both expressions are the same because of the exponents' commutativity.

If A has used the r^r protocol for registration, then A and B have to use a slightly modified KATHY protocol. It can be formalized as follows:

$$1 : A \longrightarrow B : m_A, r_A$$
$$2 : B \longrightarrow A : v_a = Y^{z_a}(\text{mod } p)$$

In this case, B generates $v_a = Y^{z_a}(\text{mod } p)$ instead of $v_a = r_A^{z_a}(\text{mod } p)$. The rest of the protocol remains the same, and A and B can both agree on the same session key $K_a = K'_a = K''_a$ by having A compute $K'_a = v_a^{s_A}(\text{mod } p)$ on the one hand, and having B compute $K''_a = (\alpha^{m_A}r_A^{-r_A})^{z_a}(\text{mod } p)$ on the other hand. At this point we want to mention that K'_a is the same as K''_a without actually showing it.

If A and B want to mutually authenticate each other, they have to run the corresponding authentication protocol in the opposite direction, too. In the case of using the basic KATHY protocol, the additional protocol steps are as follows:

$$3 : B \longrightarrow A : m_B, r_B$$
$$4 : A \longrightarrow B : v_b = r_B^{z_b}(\text{mod } p)$$

In the case of the r^r-KATHY protocol, the additional protocol steps are as follows:

$$3 : B \longrightarrow A : m_B, r_B$$
$$4 : A \longrightarrow B : v_b = Y^{z_b}(\text{mod } p)$$

In both cases, A and B can agree on another session key $K_b = K'_b = K''_b$. They can now use the following challenge-response protocol to convince themselves that they indeed posses the same session keys K_a and K_b:

$$
\begin{array}{llll}
1 : A & \longrightarrow & B : \{N_a\}K_a \\
2 : B & \longrightarrow & A : \{N_b\}K_b \\
3 : A & \longrightarrow & B : \{N_b\}K_a \\
4 : B & \longrightarrow & A : \{N_a\}K_b
\end{array}
$$

In step (1), A randomly selects a nonce N_a, encrypts it with his K_a, and sends the result to B. Similarly, B randomly selects another nonce N_b, encrypts it with his K_b, and sends the result to A in step (2). In step (3), A decrypts $\{N_b\}K_b$ with his K_b, reencrypts it with his K_a, and sends the result to B. Similarly, B decrypts $\{N_a\}K_a$ with his K_a, reencrypts it with his K_b, and sends the result to A in step (4). If at the end of the protocol, A and B both receive the same nonces as they have originally selected, they can be sure that they both posses the same session keys. They can use either K_a or K_b as a session key to provide data origin authentication, data confidentiality, and integrity services, or they can use a function f to hash the two keys to one: $K_{ab} = f(K_a, K_b)$.

Note that if A and B wanted to reauthenticate each other after a certain amount of time, they could use the same protocol without having to go through steps (1) and (3).

5.3.4 Digital Signatures

If user A has registered as described previously, he can use his public and private keys to digitally sign documents, too. If A wanted to digitally sign a message m, he would randomly select $k \in \mathbb{Z}_{p-1}^*$, compute $t = r_A^k$, and solve the congruence $m \equiv s_A t + ku \pmod{p-1}$ for u. In this case, (m, m_A, r_A, t, u) represents the authentically signed message m. The signature can be verified by checking the equation

$$
r_A^m = (\alpha^{m_A} Y^{-r_A})^t t^u
$$

For the KATHY variation using the AMV variation scheme, t must be computed as $t = Y^k$ and the congruence to solve is $m \equiv s_A u + kt \pmod{p-1}$. This leads to the verification equation

$$
Y^m = (\alpha^{m_A} r_A^{-r_A})^u t^t.
$$

Note that the verifier of such a signature only needs to be confident of the public SKIA parameters, not the parameters of each signing principal. Both digital signature schemes are incorporated into the EES application package.

5.4 DISCUSSION

In this chapter we have become acquainted with TESS, a toolbox set system of different but cooperating cryptographic mechanisms and functions based on the primitive of discrete exponentiation. The use of TESS for authentication and key distribution requires the existence of an offline SKIA that acts as a trusted third party.

Similar to a passport office, it is up to the SKIA to register new users and to provide them with credentials accordingly. A user's credentials basically consist of a self-certified public key and a corresponding private key. The usual way to provide a user with credentials is to hand over a tamper-free hardware device, such as a chipcard or personal token, and to have this hardware device store the corresponding values on the user's behalf. However, in cases where the costs of providing users with hardware devices are prohibitive, the use of plain files that are encrypted with keys that are derived from the users's passwords may be used, too.

In either case, the self-certified public keys of two arbitrary users can be used to perform a key exchange with embedded authentication. The aim of this key exchange is to end up with a secret key that can be used to subsequently protect the authenticity, confidentiality, and integrity of messages exchanged.

Recent work at the EISS has focused on the possibilities of using the discrete exponentiation for key escrow [18], and to modify the KATHY protocol to additionally support the DSS. In addition to that, a verifiable secret sharing scheme has been added to TESS, too [19]. Using this scheme, it has become feasible to securely distribute secret keys, or to build a basis to implement more sophisticated access control mechanisms to be used in distributed systems.

With regard to security management, a considerable amount of work has been dedicated to the investigation of trust relationships in arbitrary certification and SKIA hierarchies [20]. It is, in general, possible to group SKIAs hierarchically, in a way that higher level SKIAs authorize lower level SKIAs to act as such.

Mainly because of its simplicity and efficiency, TESS is an attractive authentication and key distribution system to be used in computer networks and distributed systems. However, the following points should be taken into account when evaluating the use of TESS:

1. The system is not widely deployed in terms of network applications that actually employ it. As a matter of fact, the use of SELANE in securing `telnet` access to the EISS firewall system is currently its only documented use. However, `rsh` and `rlogin` are being adapted to incorporate SELANE functionality, too.

2. The system is being developed at a university. Although this needn't be bad, in general, it is a disadvantage in terms of availability and professional support on various platforms. In particular, it should be noted that the TESS toolboxes are not freely available at the time of this writing. The EISS is yet trying to make the toolboxes publicly available as freeware, but no final decision has been made so far.

3. Having the SKIA offline avoids an obvious communication bottleneck and separates the availability of the authentication service from the availability of the corresponding servers. However, a revocation of user credentials is hard to achieve, because the SKIA(s) is (are) not involved in the actual process of authentication. Presently, revocation of credentials is only partially addressed by setting an expiration date.

TESS is currently being used in several field trials. It will be of utmost interest to study the results of these trials to further discuss the advantages and disadvantages of self-certified public keys in general, and the use of self-certified public keys in TESS in particular.

REFERENCES

[1] G.B. Agnew, R.C. Mullin, and S.A. Vanstone, "Improved Digital Signature Scheme based on Discrete Exponentiation," *Electronic Letters*, Vol. 26, 1990, pp. 1024 – 1025.

[2] D. Chaum, J.H. Evertse, and J. van de Graaf, "An Improved Protocol for Demonstrating Possession of Discrete Logarithms and some Generalizations," in D. Chaum and W.L. Price, editors, *Proceedings of EUROCRYPT '87*, Springer-Verlag, Berlin, 1988, pp. 127 – 141.

[3] Th. Beth, "Efficient Zero-Knowledge Identification Schemes for Smart Cards," in C.G. Günther, editor, *Proceedings of EUROCRYPT '88*, Springer-Verlag, Berlin, 1989, pp. 77 – 84.

[4] C.P. Schnorr, "Efficient Identification and Signatures for Smart Cards," in G. Brassard, editor, *Advances in Cryptology — CRYPTO '89*, Springer-Verlag, Berlin, 1990, pp. 240 – 251.

[5] R.L. Rivest, and A. Shamir, "How to Expose an Eavesdropper," *Communications of the ACM*, Vol. 27, 1984, pp. 393 – 395.

[6] C.G. Günther, "An Identity-Based Key-Exchange Protocol," in J.J. Quisquater and J. Vandewalle, editors, *Proceedings of EUROCRYPT '89*, Springer-Verlag, Berlin, 1990, pp. 29 – 37.

[7]   F. Bauspiess, and H.J. Knobloch, "How to Keep Authenticity Alive in a Computer Network," in J.J. Quisquater and J. Vandewalle, editors, *Proceedings of EUROCRYPT '89*, Springer-Verlag, Berlin, 1990, pp. 38 – 46.

[8]   M. Girault, "Self-certified Public Keys," in D.W. Davies, editor, *Proceedings of EURO-CRYPT '91*. Springer-Verlag, Berlin, 1991.

[9]   A. Shamir, "Identity-based Cryptosystems and Signature Schemes," in G.R. Blakley and D. Chaum, editors, *Advances in Cryptology — CRYPTO '84*, Springer-Verlag, Berlin, 1985, pp. 47 – 53.

[10] P. Horster, and H.J. Knobloch, "Discrete Logarithm Based Protocols," in D.W. Davies, editor, *Proceedings of EUROCRYPT '91*, Springer-Verlag, Berlin, 1991, pp. 399 – 408.

[11] P. Horster, and H.J. Knobloch, "Cryptographic Protocols and Network Security," *in Proceedings of IFIP SEC'92*, May 1992.

[12] T. Beth, H.J. Knobloch, S. Stempel, and P. Wichmann, "Authentifikationsdienst SELANE — Modularisierung und Einsatz," Report 94/3, University of Karlsruhe, EISS, 1994.

[13] T. Beth, and D. Gollmann, "Security Systems Based on Exponentiation Primitives: TESS — The Exponential Security System," *in Proceedings of IFIP SEC '94*, May 1994.

[14] T. Beth, "Sichere offene Datennetze," *Spektrum der Wissenschaft*, May 1995, pp. 46 – 55.

[15] H. Danisch, "The Exponential Security System TESS: An Identity-Based Cryptographic Protocol for Authenticated Key-Exchange," Request for Comments 1824, August 1995.

[16] H.J. Knobloch, and P. Horster, "Eine Krypto-Toolbox für Smartcards," *Datenschutz und Datensicherung*, Vol. 16, July 1992, pp. 353 – 361.

[17] D. Chaum, "Achieving Electronic Privacy," *Scientific American*, August 1992, pp. 96 – 101.

[18] Th. Beth, H.J. Knobloch, M. Otten, G.J. Simmons, and P. Wichmann, "Towards Acceptable Key Escrow Systems," *in Proceedings of the 2nd ACM Conference on Communications and Computing Security*, November 1994.

[19] Th. Beth, H.J. Knobloch, and M. Otten, "Verifiable Secret Sharing for Monotone Access Structures," *in Proceedings of the 1st ACM Conference on Communications and Computing Security*, November 1993.

[20] B. Klein, *Authentifikationsdienste für sichere Informationssysteme*, Ph.D. Thesis, University of Karlsruhe, Germany, November 1993.

Chapter 6

SESAME

In this chapter we focus on the European SESAME (a Secure European System for Applications in a Multivendor Environment) project. In Section 6.1 we summarize the project, and in Section 6.2 we overview the architecture of the resulting authentication and key distribution system. In Section 6.3 we briefly walk through the cryptographic protocol that SESAME is based on, and in Section 6.4 we further elaborate the applicability of the system.

6.1   PROJECT

The European Computer Manufacturer Association (ECMA[1]) was founded in 1961 to work in the field of standardization of information and communication systems. Based on the OSI security architecture and the series of corresponding security frameworks developed by the ISO/IEC JTC1 (ISO/IEC, 1989; ISO/IEC, 1993a), the ECMA published a corresponding technical report ECMA TR/46 in 1988 [1]. The report focuses on the application layer and describes a security framework in terms of application functions necessary to build distributed systems that are both open and secure. The continuation of this work led to ECMA standard 138, which specifies abstract data elements and security services that are needed in open distributed systems [2]. Similarly, ECMA standard 206 specifies a model for establishing and managing security relationships between applications in open distributed systems [3].

The ECMA has quite recently finished work to define the functionality and the protocols for a distributed security service in charge of authenticating and authorizing human and application principals, along with supportive key distribution functions. The resulting ECMA standard 219 was approved by the ECMA General Assembly in December 1994 and officially released in January 1995 [4].

SESAME[2] (a Secure European System for Applications in a Multivendor Environment) is a research and development project initiated in the wake of the ECMA work by the Commission of the European Communities (CEC). The primary objective of the project is to produce technology for support of single sign-on and access control in open distributed systems.

The SESAME project receives half of its funding from the CEC under the RACE programme (RACE R2051). The project's membership comprises both developers (including vendors) and users (including telephone companies).

SESAME was originally set up as a two-stage project:

- In stage one, the project was tasked with developing the ECMA work into a demonstrable implementation, in order to show that the architectural ideas and principles are both feasible and practical. This was achieved in 1991, and the resulting prototype implementation is commonly referred to as *SESAME V1* [5].

- In stage two, the project was tasked with developing security componentry for use in the construction of commercial security products. This stage led to the

---

[1]http://www.ecma.ch
[2]http://www.esat.kuleuven.ac.be/ vdwauver/sesame.html

development of an intermediate version called *SESAME V2* (SESAME Technology Version 2) which was released for limited beta testing to the members of the SESAME User Group and another CEC funded project in July 1994 [6]. To facilitate widespread community scrutiny and public availability of SESAME V2, a standalone toolkit on CD ROM was later released for noncommercial use, too.

Today, the end of stage two has materialized in a version called *SESAME V3* (SESAME Technology Version 3). SESAME V3 is freely available for noncommercial use, and available on licence for inclusion in commercial products.[3]

Like all CEC funded projects, SESAME is kept under scrutiny and submits to an audit process. In 1994, the work of SESAME was audited, and approval was given for continuation into 1995.

In order to conform to the ECMA security framework, SESAME V1 had to include a profile ECMA authentication service. With respect to SESAME stage two, however, the decision was made to use Kerberos V5 to allow for an easier migration from the existing installed base. SESAME V2 therefore effectively complements and builds from the capabilities provided by Kerberos V5 to enable secure transmission of privileges, and scalable interrealm key distribution by the use of public key cryptography.

In 1992, the project devoted a considerable amount of effort towards advocating the use of SESAME technology in the Open Software Foundation's (OSF) distributed computing environment (DCE). A corresponding request for comments (RFC) was submitted to the OSF in December 1992 [7].

In the following months, discussions with the OSF and its members found significant support for inclusion of SESAME technology in DCE. However, at the beginning of 1993 it became obvious that inclusion of SESAME technology could not happen for DCE version 1.1 due to resourcing constraints faced by a major DCE security technology provider. As a result, development of SESAME has continued independently from the DCE development activities since 1993. Note however that SESAME has been developed in a DCE environment, and that it is, in principle, capable of being made to coexist with DCE, as well as to work separately. As we will discuss in the subsequent chapter, several SESAME proposals were actually taken up by the OSF, and have been included into DCE.

---

[3]http://www.esat.kuleuven.ac.be/pub/COSIC/sesame3.html

The SESAME source code is collaboratively developed by

- *Bull* SA;

- *International Computers Ltd* (ICL);

- *Siemens Nixdorf Informationssysteme* (SNI) AG;

- *Software and Systems Engineering* (SSE) Ltd.

The SESAME project has adopted and slightly modified existing code implementing Kerberos, DES, RSA, and MD5. However, the project's main development effort has focused on SESAME specific extensions of Kerberos V5.

The platforms currently supported by SESAME V3 are summarized in Table 6.1. Note that client software is available for personal computers (PCs) running under MS-DOS/Windows, and that the software implementing functions for a certification authority (CA) is implemented to run on a standalone PC only.

Table 6.1
Platforms Currently Supported by SESAME V3

Platform	Client	Server	CA
Bull DPX 20 (AIX 3.2)	X	X	
SNI MX300i (SINIX)	X	X	
ICL DRS6000 (UNIX)	X	X	
IBM RS6000 (AIX 3.2)	X	X	
SunOS	X	X	
PC (MS-DOS/Windows)	X		X

Because the SESAME technology is intended to be made globally available, its source code must be issued in a form that is exportable between different nations. In order to conform with different import and export laws and corresponding controls, SESAME enables replacement of all cryptographic algorithms and one-way hash functions. In general, it is the responsibility of a company or organization contemplating use or export of the SESAME technology to obtain corresponding licenses.

The SESAME documentation is protected by a copyright that is jointly held by the developing partners Bull, ICL, SNI, and SSE. However, selected parts of the documentation that are considered to be of wider interest have been made publicly available. In particular, documentation relating to the functional specification of SESAME has been declassified by the SESAME Project Management Board and is released as needed and as appropriate to contribute to the related standardization activities.

6.2 ARCHITECTURAL OVERVIEW

The SESAME project has adopted the terminology introduced in the ISO/IEC security frameworks. In particular, it uses the term *principal* to refer to a human or system entity that is registered in and authenticatable to a system.

- When acting in an active role (for example, requesting access), a principal is called an *initiator*.

- When acting in a passive role (for example, being accessed), a principal is called a *target*.

A service is a coherent set of abstract functionality, which can be implemented as a number of separate servers. With regard to the client/server model, client application components acting as initiators communicate with server application components acting as targets.

It has already been mentioned that the primary objective of the SESAME project is to produce technology for support of single sign-on and access control in open distributed systems. Both single sign-on and access control require authentication, and an authentication service in turn offers the possibility for distributed keys that can be used to provide data confidentiality and integrity services, too. Consequently, SESAME is to provide authentication, access control, data confidentiality, and data integrity services. It achieves this by including and combining an extended Kerberos V5 authentication service, and an ECMA-style privilege attribute service:

- The *extended Kerberos V5 authentication service* supports both the normal, password-based authentication mechanism of Kerberos V5, as well as a more sophisticated authentication mechanism based on public key cryptography.

- The *ECMA-style privilege attribute service* can be used to implement role-based access control policies. The idea of having a role-based access control policy is closely related to the fact that a user working in a particular organizational role or job typically needs specific access rights. In SESAME, these access rights are called *privilege attributes* (or *privileges*), and it is generally up to a system administrator to specify both a set of privilege attributes, which is associated with a specific role, and the controls that are to apply to their use. In addition to that, the system administrator may also want to define which users can take which roles. At the beginning of a session, a user can then specify one of his roles, which should automatically give him the associated privileges.

Remember that in the basic Kerberos model a client requests a TGT from the AS, and that the client can use this TGT to request tickets from the TGS. In the SESAME model, a similar approach is used for authorization and access control. If a client wants to use a service, he must not only be authenticated by the AS, but he must also have his privilege attributes certified by a privilege attribute server (PAS). In SESAME, the term privilege attribute certificate (PAC) is used to refer to a certified set of privilege attributes. In principle, a PAC consists of both the user's privileges and corresponding control information. The user's privileges are data such as the user's identity, role, organizational group, and security clearance, whereas the control information says where and when the PAC can be used and whether it can be delegated or not. Note that a PAC is conceptually similar to an access control certificate as specified in (ISO/IEC, 1993b). In the SESAME model, a PAS generates a PAC on presentation of a proof of authentication, and the PAC is digitally signed with the private key of the corresponding PAS.

If one simplified the SESAME model beyond what is legitimate, one could look at it as illustrated in Figure 6.1. Note at this point that this SESAME model is very similar to the Kerberos model. The most obvious differences are that the PAS is added as a third component to the security server and that the TGS is named key distribution server (KDS) in the SESAME model.

In short, a client first requests a PAS ticket from the extended Kerberos V5 AS. If the client gets the ticket, he uses it to request a PAC and a ticket for the KDS from the PAS. If the client receives both the PAC and the KDS ticket, he uses it to obtain a service ticket and the keying information that is needed to use the ticket. Finally, the client can authenticate to the server, and if mutual authentication is required, the server can authenticate to the client, too.

The messages that are exchanged between the client and the security and application servers are enumerated in Figure 6.1. The numbers match to the corresponding SESAME protocol steps that are summarized in Table 6.2. Note that after step 7 or 8, a security context is established between the client and the application server. They can now send and receive SES_DATA messages that are cryptographically protected. These additional protocol steps are neither shown in Figure 6.1

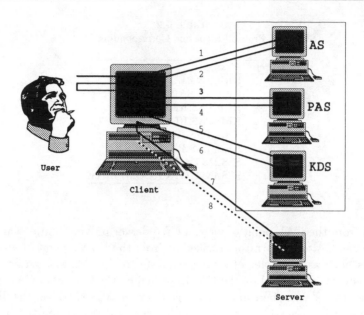

Figure 6.1   A simplified view of the SESAME model.

nor enumerated in Table 6.2.

The architecture of SESAME V3 is actually more complicated than the simplified view shown in Figure 6.1. In a SESAME domain, the AS, PAS, and KDS are typically processes that are running on one particular host, and this host is commonly referred to as the SESAME domain security server (DSS).

A DSS maintains a security management information base (SMIB), which stores all security-related data on behalf of the AS, PAS, and KDS. In addition to that, every SESAME security domain also runs a local registration authority (LRA) server that users can contact to get information from the certification authority (CA). Note that SESAME V3 uses public key cryptography, and that it must therefore provide a possibility to generate and distribute public key certificates.

In SESAME V3, the CA is assumed to run in a domain of its own, and this domain may not have any relation to other SESAME security domains. Also, the CA may work offline, and may not be accessible directly from the network. Instead, links between the online LRAs and the offline CA are established through offline certificate authority agent (CAA) servers that are located in the CA domain.

Table 6.2
SESAME Protocol Steps and Corresponding Messages.

Step	Message
1	KRB_AS_REQ
2	KRB_AS_REP
3	KRB_PAS_REQ
4	KRB_PAS_REP
5	KRB_TGS_REQ
6	KRB_TGS_REP
7	SES_INIT_CTXT
8	SES_INIT_CTXT_COMPLETE

Looked at from the CA's point of view, a CAA server provides data to and receives data from the CA administrator. Looked at from the LRA's point of view, a CAA server acts both as a spooler of signed requests to the CA, and an agent for the supply of key pairs certified by the CA. In principle, the CA and a CAA server can use any file transfer mechanism to exchange data. In SESAME V3, the file transfer is performed using removable media, such as floppy disks, supported by both the machine supporting the CAA and the machine supporting the CA.

The different security servers and security domains in SESAME V3 are illustrated in Figure 6.2. The dotted oval on the top represents the CA domain, whereas the two dotted rectangles on the bottom represent two SESAME security domains. On the one hand, the CA domain consists of an offline CA, an online CAA server, and an asynchronous communication line between them. On the other hand, every SESAME security domain consists of a DSS and a LRA server, with the DSS actually consisting of an AS, PAS, and KDS. The connection between the LRA and the CAA in the CA domain is established through a synchronous communications line.

From a network application's point of view, the architecture of SESAME V3 is illustrated in Figure 6.3. Let's assume an application client running on the initiator machine on the left side seeks to authenticate to an application server running on the target machine on the right side. Both the initiator and the target machine may (but need not) be registered in the same SESAME security domain.

There are several architectural components involved in the SESAME model, and the following components must be installed on the initiator' side:

- The user sponsor (US) provides a user interface to the system. In SESAME V3, only a minimal command line US is provided. It allows the user to login

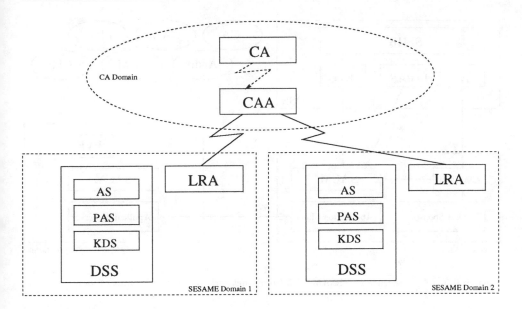

Figure 6.2   Security servers and security domains in SESAME V3.

(`seslogin`), to change privileges and control attributes (`chattr`), and to logout
by cleaning up the user's cached privileges and control attributes obtained during
a session (`seslogout`). It is assumed that the US would in practice be replaced
by a vendor-specific and more sophisticated component.

- The authentication and privilege attribute (APA) client is the architectural component used by the US to hide from it the details of initial authentication and
  default PAC acquisition.

- In general, the secure association context manager (SACM) is in charge of establishing and maintaining a security context between a client and a server of
  one particular application. The *initiator SACM* is the SACM component on the
  initiator' side.

Obviously, a SACM component must be installed on the target side, too, and
this component is referred to as *target SACM*. The target SACM is supported by
a PAC validation facility (PVF). As discussed further below, the PVF checks the
validity of a PAC and returns the dialogue keys that are needed to secure the

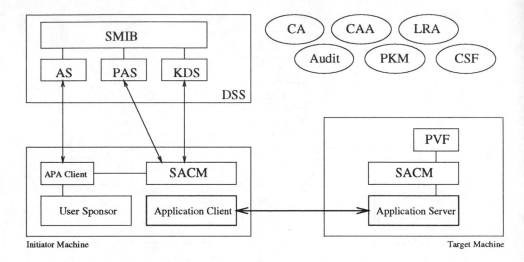

Figure 6.3   Architecture of SESAME V3 from a network application's point of view.

conversation with an initiator. For this purpose, the PVF knows the public key of the PAS, and also shares a secret key with the DSS. If a digital signature in a PAC is not recognized, the PVF calls the SESAME inter domain service (IDS) to provide a suitable PAC instead. In short, the IDS is responsible for delivering a certified set of security attributes for the target domain on presentation of a verified set of attributes from the initiator domain.

In addition to these components that are installed either on the initiator or target side, there are three generic components that are required in a number of different places within the overall picture of SESAME V3:

1. The public key management (PKM) consists of a linked-in library providing access to various certificate and key handling functions, as well as a set of command line administration tools that can be used, for example, to generate and revoke keys of a public key cryptosystem.

2. The cryptographic support facility (CSF) implements cryptographic algorithms that are used either by SESAME components or SESAME supported applications. The algorithms that are currently implemented and used in SESAME V3 are DES-CBC, RSA, MD5, and DES-MD5. Note however that the CSF has been designed so that algorithms can be replaced and key sizes adjusted according to

local legislation or emergence of better algorithms in the future. Also note that for export control reasons, the public version of SESAME V3 uses a simple key-dependent XOR function to encrypt user data, and that only commercial versions include the DES and another secret key cryptosystem.

3. Audit events are security-relevant actions that occur in a system and are worthy of recording for subsequent analysis. In SESAME V3, an audit facility logs audit events via a write-only pipe to an audit daemon that runs under its own user identification and that stores the audit information in a corresponding file. The audit file is thereby protected from modification by application processes. In SESAME V3, the components that audit activities are the KDS, PVF, initiator and target SACMs, and APA client. Retrieval and analysis of this information is out of the scope of SESAME. However, it is expected that separate tools will be developed to take advantage of the audit files.

SESAME uses a two-level key hierarchy that consists of basic and dialogue keys.

- A *basic key* is established and used between an initiator SACM and the PVF of a target SACM to protect the corresponding PACs and key establishment information;

- A *dialogue key* is derived from a basic key using a one-way hash function. The dialogue key is to protect data that is exchanged in a security context. Separate dialogue keys can be established for confidentiality and integrity protection, enabling different strengths of mechanisms to be used to conform with local regulations.

With respect to application programming, SESAME V3 conforms and partly extends the GSS-API (compare Appendix A). Table 6.3 summarizes the implementation status of the GSS-API base calls, and Table 6.4 summarizes the implementation status of the GSS-API extension calls. The first group of GSS-API extension calls (1 to 4) protect application dialogues, whereas the second group (5 to 9) deals with security attributes and delegation extensions.

6.3   CRYPTOGRAPHIC PROTOCOL

Having Figure 6.1 and Table 6.2 in mind, we now briefly walk through the cryptographic protocol that SESAME V3 is based on. However, instead of formalizing the protocol we are going to use a verbal description.

Table 6.3

Implementation Status of the GSS-API Base Calls in SESAME V3

GSS-API Call	Status
GSS_Acquire_cred()	Fully supported
GSS_Release_cred()	Fully supported
GSS_Inquire_cred()	Partly supported
GSS_Init_sec_context()	Partly supported
GSS_Accept_sec_context()	Fully supported
GSS_Delete_sec_context()	Fully supported
GSS_Process_context_token()	Fully supported
GSS_Context_time()	Fully supported
GSS_Display_status()	Fully supported
GSS_Indicate_mechs()	Fully supported
GSS_Compare_name()	Fully supported
GSS_Display_name()	Fully supported
GSS_Import_name()	Fully supported
GSS_Release_name()	Fully supported
GSS_Release_buffer()	Fully supported
GSS_Release_oid_set()	Fully supported

When a user walks up to a client workstation to log in, he has to provide the user sponsor (US) with name, password, and requested role. The US forwards this information to the APA client and in step (1) of the SESAME protocol, the APA client sends a KRB_AS_REQ message to the AS requesting a TGT. The format of the KRB_AS_REQ message is essentially the same as in the Kerberos protocol. The AS generates a PAS ticket and a corresponding basic key, and returns a KRB_AS_REP message to the APA client in step (2).

The Kerberos AS exchange thus results in acquisition of a PAS ticket and a corresponding basic key, which are deposited with the SACM on the initiator side. From now on, all the interactions between the client and the DSS are performed by the initiator SACM.

In step (3) of the SESAME protocol, the initiator SACM sends a KRB_PAS_REQ message to the PAS. The message includes both the PAS ticket and the required user role. Taking into account the required user role, the PAS generates a PAC, digitally signs it with his private key, and additionally generates a KDS ticket.

In step (4), the PAS returns a KRB_PAS_REP message to the initiator SACM, and this message includes both the PAC and the KDS ticket. In addition to that, the message may also include control values (CVs) that are needed if the PAC is

Table 6.4

Implementation Status of the GSS-API Extension Calls in SESAME V3

GSS-API Call	Status
GSS_Get_mic()	Partly supported
GSS_Verify_mic()	Fully supported
GSS_Wrap()	Partly supported
GSS_Unwrap()	Fully supported
GSS_Modify_cred()	Fully supported
GSS_Get_attributes()	Fully supported
GSS_Compound_cred()	Nonfunctionally supported
GSS_Get_delegate_creds()	Nonfunctionally supported
GSS_Set_default_cred()	Fully supported

delegatable. The KRB_PAS_REP message is encrypted with the basic key that the initiator SACM shares with the PAS.

The initiator SACM caches all information that he has received so far, namely the PAS and KDC tickets, the PAC, the CVs, and the basic key. A user-handling program can now access the attributes present in the PAC through corresponding API calls, so that, for example, a user can be informed of what privileges he's currently working with. Provided that these initialization steps have been carried out successfully, any application client on the initiator' side can invoke the SACM component through corresponding GSS-API calls. If for any reason the PAC cached by the SACM is not valid or not appropriate, the SACM requests a new PAC from the PAS.

If a client wants to use a specific application server on the target side, he has the initiator SACM request a corresponding ticket by sending a KRB_TGS_REQ message to the KDS in step (5). If the KDS shares a secret key with the PVF of the corresponding target SACM, the KDS returns a KRB_TGS_REP message to the initiator SACM in step (6). The message not only includes a service ticket for the requested target application server, but the corresponding keying material as well.

In step (7), the initiator SACM generates a SES_INIT_CTXT message that contains the service ticket, a dialogue key package containing confidentiality and integrity key seeds, and the PAC. When the application protocol conveys the context establishment token from the initiator SACM to the target SACM, the latter forwards it to his PVF for verification. The PVF processes the keying information to extract the basic key, and uses the dialogue key package to generate two dialogue keys, namely a confidentiality dialogue key and an integrity dialogue key. If the ticket is valid, and if mutual authentication is required, the target SACM returns a SES_INIT_CTXT_COMPLETE message to the initiator SACM in step (8). A security context is now established between the initiator and target SACM, and any application can use this security context for data transmission. As a matter of fact, any data being transmitted in SES_DATA messages is sequence-protected and integrity-protected, and may, subject to policy, be confidentiality-protected, too. After the application has completed, and when context termination is requested, a SES_CTXT_ABORT message is sent to request a termination.

6.4   DISCUSSION

In this chapter we have shown how the work in the SESAME project has extended the Kerberos authentication and key distribution system to use public key cryptography, and how the use of public key cryptography can provide advantages in terms of scalability and manageability. The resulting authentication and key distribution system, namely SESAME V3, not only provides authentication, data confidentiality, and integrity services, but authorization and access control services, too. Consequently, SESAME provides an intersting alternative to Kerberos. Another advantage of SESAME is due to the fact that the system is not a proprietary development. Instead, it has its roots in the standards work of the ECMA and is not tied to any specific system platform or communication protocol suite. From the very beginning, the SESAME authentication and key distribution system has been designed for a multivendor environment, and this design objective pays off when it comes to an integration of the system in large organizations or clusters of cooperating organizations. It is thus assumed that we will see more Sesamized applications in the near future.

REFERENCES

[1] ECMA, "Security in Open Systems — A Security Framework," ECMA TR/46, European Computer Manufacturer Association, Geneva, Switzerland, July 1988.

[2] ECMA, "Security in Open Systems — Data Elements and Service Definitions," ECMA Standard 138, European Computer Manufacturer Association, Geneva, Switzerland, December 1989.

[3] ECMA, "Association Context Management including Security Context Management," ECMA Standard 206, European Computer Manufacturer Association, Geneva, Switzerland, December 1993.

[4] ECMA, "Authentication and Privilege Attribute Security Application with Related Key Distribution Functions — Part 1, 2 and 3," ECMA Standard 219, European Computer Manufacturer Association, Geneva, Switzerland, December 1994.

[5] T.A. Parker, "A Secure European System for Applications in a Multi-vendor Environment (The SESAME Project)," *in Proceedings of the 14th National Computer Security Conference*, 1991.

[6] P.V. McMahon, "SESAME V2 Public Key and Authorisation Extensions to Kerberos," *in Proceedings of the Internet Society Symposium on Network and Distributed System Security*, February 1995, pp. 114 – 131.

[7] S.B. Fairthorne, "Security Extensions for DCE 1.1," OSF DCE SIG Request for Comments: 19.0, December 1992.

Chapter 7

OSF DCE

The Open Software Foundation's (OSF) distributed computing environment (DCE) is an integrated suite of tools and services that support the development and use of distributed applications. The aim of this chapter is to focus on OSF DCE in general, and the DCE security service in particular. In Section 7.1 we briefly summarize the development of the system, and in Section 7.2 we overview its architecture. In Sections 7.3 and 7.4 we then describe and further discuss the cryptographic protocols that the DCE security service implements.

7.1 DEVELOPMENT

The Open Software Foundation (OSF[1]) was founded in 1988 as a consortium of companies who wanted to cooperate in the development of software for the open systems market. The OSF headquarter is located in Cambridge, Massachusetts, and several OSF offices are distributed throughout in the United States, the Pacific Region, and Europe.

The mode of operation is as follows: When the OSF decides to become active in a certain field, it publishes a corresponding request for technology (RFT). A RFT

---

[1]http://www.osf.org/index.html

invites the members of the OSF to submit technology proposals. The proposals are thoroughly reviewed and evaluated by the OSF. Based on the evaluation results, the OSF selects one (or more) companie(s) to develop the requested software, and to provide both the source code and the documentation to the OSF. The OSF then distributes the software among its member organizations. If a member organization decides to license the software, it receives the source code and the documentation from the OSF, but still has to port the software to its own platform(s), package a corresponding product, sell it, and return royalties to the OSF. On the other side, the OSF has to provide a certain percentage of the money that it receives from its licensees to those companies that originally developed the software.

When the OSF decided to become active in the field of distributed computing, it published an RFT for a distributed computing environment (DCE). The OSF member organizations were invited to submit DCE proposals until October 1989, and most of the proposals were submitted by

- *Digital Equipment Corporation* (DEC);

- *Hewlett-Packard Company* (HP);

- *International Business Machines Corporation* (IBM);

- *Siemens Nixdorf Informationssysteme* (SNI) AG;

- Transarc Corporation.

In 1990, the OSF reviewed and evaluated the submitted proposals, and made its decisions. The selected proposals were integrated into a fully operable system, and this system was specified in a set of application environment specifications (AESs), which was officially released in 1992.

Note that the AESs are public. In principle, anybody can follow the AESs and implement a fully operable DCE system from the scratch. However, most DCE providers license the source code and documentation from the OSF, and port the software to their own platform(s). Since 1992, DCE has been ported to most platforms in use today, and the OSF maintains a *DCE product listing* that contains information pertaining to products and services related to DCE. The DCE product listing can be ordered directly from one of the OSF offices.

Further information about DCE in general, and the security mechanisms in particular can be found in [1 – 3]. *Bell Communications Research* (Bellcore) has analyzed the security of the DCE, and a corresponding "OSF DCE Security Analysis Report" is available from Bellcore, too.[2]

7.2 ARCHITECTURAL OVERVIEW

OSF DCE has already been introduced as an integrated suite of tools and services that support the development and use of distributed applications. The goal of DCE is to turn a computer network into a single, coherent computing engine. As a layer of software that masks differences among different kinds of computers, DCE sits on the top of the host and network operating systems, and offers its services to the applications above. In particular, DCE allows and supports the development and use of distributed applications that can tap into a network's latent power using widespread resources. Because distributed parts of these applications can execute concurrently, they can, in general, be made more efficient than single-processor applications that must act on data sequentially.

In DCE, an administration domain is called a *cell*. A DCE cell consists of a group of users, systems, and resources that have a common purpose and share common services. It typically consists of nodes in a restricted geographic area, but geography does not necessarily determine the boundaries of a cell. Factors that can also determine the boundaries of a DCE cell include an organization's size, its network topology, as well as its needs and preferences.

In a decentralized and distributed environment, it is important to be able to locate resources, to keep the systems synchronized, and to provide various security services. Consequently, DCE provides a set of integrated services that work across multiple systems and remain independent of single systems. The core DCE services are

- A *directory service*;

- A *distributed time service* (DTS);

- A *security service*.

At a minimum, a DCE cell configuration must include these core services. Distributed application clients usually find their application servers by looking up information posted in the directory service. Application servers determine the authenticity and authorization level of clients by using highly protected information

---

[2]http://www.bellcore.com/SECURITY/osfdce.html

from the security service, and the security service uses time information from the DTS to limit the lifespan of security-related information.

In addition to the three core services, a typical DCE cell configuration also offers additional services, such as a distributed file service (DFS). All DCE services are integrated with *DCE Threads* and *RPC* (remote procedure call):

- Threads are the most fundamental components in DCE. As a matter of fact, DCE needs to be able to run multiple threads of process execution simultaneously on the involved machines to facilitate things like asynchronous input/output and concurrent servicing. Since many operating systems do not inherently support multithreaded execution, a user-level threading package is included with DCE that is compliant with POSIX 1003.4a. The DCE Threads package gives users the ability to create, schedule, synchronize, and otherwise manage multiple threads in a single process.

- RPC is layered on top of DCE Threads. All DCE services are based on RPC. In principle, RPC calls are function calls outside of a host's address space that look and taste like local procedure calls.

A *DCE client host* is a DCE host that runs an application client or an application server but does not run a DCE server. Similarly, a *DCE server host* is a DCE host that runs one or more DCE servers. A DCE client host has the necessary DCE client software to interact with DCE servers and other DCE clients in the cell. Note that DCE server hosts also contain the DCE client software because they may need to interact with DCE servers located on other hosts and with other DCE client hosts, too.

A DCE runtime library must be on every DCE host regardless of whether the host is a client or server. The library includes DCE Threads and RPC routines, as well as some other routines that are needed for DCE operations. In the following sections, we have a closer look at the three DCE core services.

7.2.1   Directory Service

Distributed computing involves the interaction of multiple systems to do work that is done on one system in a centralized computing environment. One challenge that arises from this new environment is the need for a universally consistent way to identify and locate resources. The usual approach to address this challenge is to use a directory service. A directory service is much like a telephone directory assistance service that provides a phone number when given a subsciber's name. Given a unique name of a resource, it is up to the directory service to return the network address of the resource along with other information related to the name.

In general, a naming environment provides a universally consistent way to name resources anywhere in a distributed environment. In DCE, universal unique identifiers (UUIDs) are used to uniquely identify resources, and the *DCE Directory Service* is to store and manage these UUIDs as well as to control the naming environment accordingly. The DCE directory service includes both

- A *cell directory service* (CDS);

- A *global directory service* (GDS).

The CDS controls the naming environment inside a cell, whereas the GDS controls the naming environment outside and between DCE cells. When the CDS determines that a name is outside the current DCE cell, it passes the name to a global name server agent outside the cell using an intermediary called global directory agent (GDA). The GDA makes cell interaction possible. It enables CDS to access a name in another cell using either of the global naming schemes (GDS or DNS).

Note that the GDS is an implementation of the ITU-T X.500 directory service, whereas the domain name service (DNS) is another name service that is most widely deployed within the Internet community. The point is that although DNS is not part of the DCE technology offering, the DCE directory service does contain support for cells to address each other through DNS.

7.2.2   Distributed Time Service

In computer networks and distributed systems, applications typically use time to control operations. As long as the clocks controlling events are properly synchronized, either with real time or with related events, applications can execute smoothly. However, problems occur, when clocks are not synchronized. Clock synchronization is thus a fundamental requirement in computer networks and distributed systems.

The DCE distributed time service (DTS) supports clock synchronization within a DCE cell. In principle, DTS itself is a RPC-based client/server application. Each DCE cell has one or more DTS servers that provide time information to client hosts and applications through intermediaries called clerks. DTS clerks interact with DTS servers, relieving client applications from this work. Each host that is not a DTS server has at least a DTS clerk. Because no device can measure the exact time at a particular instant, DTS servers and clerks express the time as an interval containing the correct time.

- Clerks obtain time intervals from several DTS servers and compute the intersection at which the intervals overlap. They adjust the system clocks of their client systems to the midpoint of the computed intersection. When they receive a time interval that does not intersect with the majority, they declare the nonintersecting value to be faulty. In general, clerks ignore faulty values when computing new times, thereby ensuring that defective DTS servers do not affect clients.

- DTS servers synchronize themselves by obtaining time information from all other DTS servers within a cell. Like clerks, servers also compute the intersection at which the intervals overlap and adjust their host clocks to the midpoint of the computed intersection.

Note that the DTS ensures that DCE hosts share a consistent notion of time, but that this time need not necessarily be the correct time. In order to make sure that the time used to synchronize DCE hosts is correct, DTS servers can synchronize with external time standards by setting the time manually or by connecting to an external time service provider.

7.2.3   Security Service

Similar to other distributed environments, security services must be built into DCE applications so that clients can call local security routines to acquire credentials that may be passed to servers, and servers can call security routines to verify these credentials. The *DCE security service* comprises three security services:

- An *authentication service*;

- An *authorization* or *privilege service*;

- A *registry service*.

In short, the authentication service provides mutual authentication for clients and servers, the authorization or privilege service supplies authorization information about a client, and the registry service maintains a database of all the principal, group, and account information for a DCE cell, as well as information about the cell itself. In principle, the DCE registry service is analogous to the central database in Kerberos, or to the /etc/passwd and /etc/group files in a UNIX system. The infomation stored in the DCE registry is used by both the authentication and authorization services, as well as any DCE application. Let's have a closer look at the DCE authentication and authorization services next.

Authentication Service

In DCE, principals are users, servers, cells, and hosts. Users are principals because the identity of the user that initiates an action, such as an RPC call, is needed to determe whether access should be granted. Servers are principals because they need to authenticate the client that initiates an action on the user's behalf, and because the client may want to authenticate a server, too. Cells are principals because two cells can exchange secret keys to support intercell authentication. And last, but not least, hosts are principals, too, because there are cases where they must authenticate the DCE security service itself. The fact that hosts are considered as principals in DCE is indeed one of the major differences between the Kerberos and the DCE security model.

Thanks to the DCE directory service every principal has a *principal name*. This principal name can be expressed as a global or cell-relative name. For example, `/.../cell_A/oppliger` is the global name of a principal, whereas `oppliger` is the corresponding cell-relative name. The use of global names makes it possible to unambiguously specify principals regardless of the cells from which the names are encountered. However, principal names can change, and what remains constant for every principal is only its UUID. Consequently, DCE uses UUIDs when credentials are passed around, and these UUIDs are mapped to principal names only when needed. Note that the split between the name and the UUID is similar to the situation in a UNIX system where every user has both a username and a user identification (UID).

We have briefly mentioned in Chapter 2 that the *DCE authentication service* was built upon the MIT reference implementation of Kerberos V5. We are not going to repeat the description and discussion of Kerberos in this chapter. However, there are two major differences between Kerberos V5 and the DCE authentication service that we want to emphazise at this point:

- The DCE authentication service is able to interpret both DCE principal names and Kerberos principal names.

- Kerberos uses UDP/IP while DCE in addition uses DCE RPC for communications. More precisely, Kerberos clients send ticket requests to a well-known UDP port and receive responses back in UDP/IP datagrams. The equivalent operations in DCE, however, are performed by using RPCs. In other respects, the DCE authentication service is compatible with Kerberos V5 and, in fact, can receive requests from Kerberos clients over UDP/IP. This means that a DCE authentication service, in principle, can replace an AS in existing Kerberos installations.

Since the reference implementation of the DCE authentication service uses the Kerberos V5 source code, the native Kerberos API still exists. However, the Kerberos API is not made available to applications. DCE version 1.0.x does not even support an API to the authentication service. Instead, the use of the authentication service is integrated with the DCE login and RPC facilities. DCE applications invoke the authentication service indirectly when they login and when they make use of authenticated RPC. Since DCE version 1.1, the GSS-API is supported to allow non-RPC applications to use DCE authentication and authorization, too.

Authorization Service

With regard to the *DCE authorization* or *privilege service*, the OSF has adapted a SESAME-like approach: priviledge attribute certificates (PACs) are issued by a dedicated server to carry the principal's security attributes that are used to make access control decisions. The security attributes of a principal basically consist of the principal's identity and some group-related information. In spite of their functional similarities, however, the format of a DCE PAC differs from the format of a SESAME PAC. A DCE version 1 PAC is illustrated in Figure 7.1.

In the DCE PAC, an *authentication flag* shows whether the certificate was authenticated by the DCE security service. This flag is necessary because, in principle, clients can also supply unauthenticated PACs. The next field, namely the *Cell UUID*, is the UUID of the principal's home cell, (i.e., the cell in whose registry the principal is registered). This field is followed by the *principal UUID*, which is the UUID of the principal whose security attributes are certified by the PAC. The rest of the PAC describes the various groups to which the principal may belong. Although a distinction is made between local and foreign groups, DCE currently supports only local groups. Local groups are groups registered in the principal's home cell. For purposes of access control, all the local groups are treated the same. Consequently, a principal will be granted access if any of his groups are authorized. For administrative purposes, one of these groups is the primary gorup. This is the group whose UUID is stored in the *primary group UUID* field of the PAC. The other local groups are stored in the variable-length *secondary group UUIDs* field

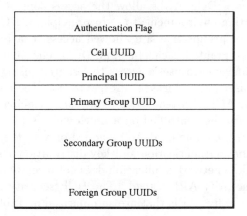

Authentication Flag
Cell UUID
Principal UUID
Primary Group UUID
Secondary Group UUIDs
Foreign Group UUIDs

Figure 7.1   DCE version 1 priviledge attribute certificate (PAC).

that follows the primary group UUID field. The last part of a PAC comprises a *foreign group UUIDs* field. Each entry in this list specifies a foreign cell UUID as well as a foreign group UUID. As mentioned previously, the current version of DCE does not support foreign groups. Consequently, this field is always empty in DCE version 1.0 and 1.1.

Remember that Kerberos V5 has a reserved authorization data field in the tickets it uses. Consequently, the DCE authentication service inherits this data field. It can be used by the DCE authorization service to place a PAC. As a matter of fact, when a client requests a TGT from the AS, he receives a TGT with an empty authorization data field. It is then up to the client, to have the DCE authorization service place a PAC (DCE version 1.0) or an extended PAC (EPAC) or a Version 2 PAC (DCE version 1.1) in the TGT. A TGT with a PAC or EPAC in its authorization data field is called a privilege ticket granting ticket (PTGT). When the client receives a PTGT, he can request the authentication service for a specific service ticket. In this case, the authentication service simply copies the authorization data field of the PTGT into the authorization data field of the *privilege ticket* (PT) that it generates.

In DCE, a discretionnary access control (DAC) policy is enforced by using access control lists (ACLs). DCE ACLs form a superset of the ACLs specified by the POSIX 1003.6 ACL working group. Note that POSIX ACLs were primarily designed to control file access of users sharing a single computer system. In particular, they restrict inclusion to members within one organization, and are applicable only to files. The extensions of DCE ACLs allow the access control lists to be useful in a distributed computing environment, too. In principle, a DCE ACL includes the names of principals or groups that are allowed access to a resource and specifies which permissions are granted each. In large DCE cells, it is usually impractical to independently manage each user's access to resources using his or her principal name. Each time a user joins or leaves an organization, the name has to be added or deleted from many ACLs. Instead, by making each principal a member of one or more groups, access can be controlled on a much wider scale. Each time a person joins an organization, the name needs to be added only to the desired group.

Similar to the other authentication and key distribution systems described and discussed in this book, a network application does not directly call the DCE security service, but uses a security API instead. The DCE security API is extensive. It basically consists of the five APIs that are summarized in Table 7.1.

Table 7.1
DCE Security APIs

API	Scope
Authenticated RPC API	Allows clients and servers to establish secure communications and transmit security attributes.
Sec_login API	Allows principals to set up their DCE identity and security attributes.
Key management API	Allows servers to manage their secret keys.
Registry API	Offers access to information stored in the security registry.
Sec_acl API	Allows management applications to control remote access control lists (ACLs).

It is useful to group the five APIs into three categories (client, server, and management applications) to indicate who is most likely to use a particular API. The authenticated RPC API is used by both clients and servers, the sec_login API and key management APIs are used primarily by servers, and the registry and sec_acl APIs are used primarily by management applications.

Is is important to note that the GSS-API takes a different approach from authenticated RPC. In particular, the GSS-API explicitly separates out the security mechanisms and relies upon the application to transfer all security and encrypted data to its peer, whereas authenticated RPC integrates security with communications. To provide interoperability with Kerberized applications, a superset of the GSS-API has been incorporated into DCE 1.1, too. The DCE security APIs and the DCE GSS-API are not further discussed in this book. An introduction into DCE security programming and the use of the DCE Security and GSS-APIs can be found in [4, 5].

7.3 CRYPTOGRAPHIC PROTOCOLS

In this section we focus on the cryptographic protocols that the DCE security service implements. In doing so, we can profit from the work we have done in previous chapters. As a matter of fact, the cryptographic protocols that the DCE security service implements are basically the Kerberos V5 protocol for authentication and name-based authorization, and a SESAME-like enhancement for PAC-based authorization.

7.3.1 Name-Based Authorization

The DCE security service is based on Kerberos V5 for authentication and name-based authorization. Consequently, we are not going to repeat the corresponding protocol, but refer to section 2.3.3 instead.

At this point we only want to emphasize that prior to version 1.2 there has been no interoperability commitment in the DCE offering. Because the Kerberos V5 protocol has become more stable with the release of RFC 1510 and its movement through the IETF standards process, DCE version 1.2 enhances the high degree of interoperability that existed in previous releases with committed support for the RFC 1510 protocol. This support will formally allow Kerberos V5 applications running on either DCE or non-DCE platforms to access the DCE security server as a RFC 1510 Kerberos server.

7.3.2 PAC-Based Authorization

The basic idea of PAC-based authorization in DCE is to have a privilege server (PS) that is coupled with the DCE registry service to generate authorization data fields in TGTs, and to have Kerberos copy these data fields from PTGTs to PTs.

With PAC-based authorization, a user logs in just like in normal Kerberos or DCE with name-based authorization. The client, acting on the user's behalf, gets an ordinary Kerberos TGT with the user's name inside. The client then asks the TGS to be provided with a ticket for the PS. Note at this point that to the TGS, the PS is just another server principal in the same realm. Equipped with a corresponding ticket, the client can contact the PS. The PS extracts the user's name from the ticket, looks up the user's UUID and group membership, and requests a TGT from the KDC with the PS' name in the client name field, and the user's UUID and group membership in the authorization data field. As mentioned previously, this TGT is referred to as a privilege TGT (PTGT). The PS then returns to the client the PTGT and the corresponding session key instead of the original TGT. From now on, the client can use the PTGT instead of the TGT.

Note that PAC-based authorization is not generally less efficient than name-based authorization. As a matter of fact, all steps until the client receives the PTGT must be performed only once. Afterwards, the client can use the PTGT to request as many PTs as he likes. The remaining steps to request a ticket and to authenticate to the corresponding server are essentially the same for both name-based and PAC-based authorization.

7.4   DISCUSSION

In this chapter we have focused on the Open Software Foundation's (OSF) distributed computing environment (DCE) in general, and the DCE security service in particular. The DCE security service consists of three components, namely an authentication service that conforms to Kerberos V5, an authorization or privilege service that is similar to the SESAME PAS, and a registry service. In principle, the DCE authorization service enhances the authentication service by adding PACs to TGTs and tickets. PACs provide the security attributes that are used by the servers to mediate access control. This way, an application server gets both authentication and authorization information in the same ticket when it receives a DCE RPC call. Once the server has obtained this information, it can use its access control list to decide whether the client should be granted access or not.

The Kerberos reference implementations from MIT have traditionally integrated network applications, such as `telnet`, `rlogin`, and `ftp`, to achieve a single sign-on facility in a network environment. Earlier versions of DCE have not followed this example, and have not included these utilities accordingly. However, DCE version 1.2 is expected to fill this gap, and to include implementations of these applications that actually use DCE name-based authentication, too.

In addition to that, DCE version 1.2 will also be able to support public key cryptography for login. Using this technology, the DCE security service need not store a long term secret key (or password) for every principal, but can use public keys instead. The system will allow some principals to use DCE 1.0 and 1.1 authentication mechanisms, and others to use public key-based authentication mechanisms. DCE version 1.2 will retain interoperability with existing DCE releases in this respect.

At login, public key users will receive credentials that allow them to use the current name-based authentication mechanism. The DCE 1.1 preauthentication protocol as specified in [6] is used so that the login client need not determine whether a given user is using public key cryptography prior to requesting credentials. Further details on the use of public key cryptography in DCE 1.2 can be found in [7].

REFERENCES

[1] W. Rosenberry, W. Kenney, and G. Fisher, *Understanding DCE*, Sebastopol, CA: O'Reilly & Associates, Inc., 1992.

[2] A. Schill, *DCE — The OSF Distributed Computing Environment*, Berlin: Springer-Verlag, 1993.

[3] A. Grossmann, "Analyse und Beurteilung des OSF DCE Sicherheitssystems," Diplomarbeit, Universität Bern, 1995.

[4] W. Hu, *DCE Security Programming*, Sebastopol, CA: O'Reilly & Associates, Inc., 1995.

[5] J. Wray, "GSS-API Extensions for DCE," OSF DCE SIG Request for Comments: 5.2, March 1994.

[6] J. Pato, "Using Pre-authentication to avoid Password Guessing Attacks," OSF DCE SIG Request for Comments: 26.0, June 1993.

[7] A. Anderson and J. Wray, "DCE 1.2 Public Key Login — Functional Specification," OSF DCE SIG Request for Comments: 68.1, February 1993.

Chapter 8

Comparison

The authentication and key distribution systems that have been described and discussed in this book differ in various respects. In this chapter, we focus on the security services they provide, the cryptographic techniques they use, the standards they conform to, and their availability and exportability.

8.1 SECURITY SERVICES

The authentication and key distribution systems don't provide the same sets of security services, and the situation is summarized in Table 8.1. In the table headings, the term AU is used to refer to authentication services, DC to data confidentiality services, DI to data integrity services, AC to access control services, and NR to nonrepudiation services. An X in the table indicates that the authentication and key distribution system mentioned in the line provides the security services mentioned in the column.

Obviously, all authentication and key distribution systems provide authentication services. In addition to that, all systems provide data confidentiality and integrity services. Note however that NetSP uses CDMF to provide data confidentiality services, and that CDMF is a DES variant with a reduced key length of

Table 8.1
Security Services Provided by the Systems

System	AU	DC	DI	AC	NR
Kerberos	X	X	X		
NetSP	X	(X)	X		
SPX	X	X	X		
TESS	X	X	X		X
SESAME	X	X	X	X	
OSF DCE	X	X	X	X	

40 bits. You can argue that this key length is sufficient enough to provide data confidentiality services, but you can also argue that the contrary is true. To avoid any discussion about the cryptographical strength of 40 bit keys, the X for NetSP providing data confidentiality services is put in parentheses in Table 8.1.

In addition to authentication, data confidentiality, and data integrity services, TESS, SESAME and OSF DCE provide some additional functionality, too. In particular, TESS is able to provide non-repudiation services due to its use of ElGamal signatures, and both SESAME and OSF DCE are able to provide authorization and access control services due to their use of privilege attribute certificates.

8.2 CRYPTOGRAPHIC TECHNIQUES

The authentication and key distribution system not only provide different security services, but they also use different cryptographic techniques to provide these services. The situation is shown in Table 8.2. In the table headings, the term *OWHF* is used to refer to one-way hash function, *SKC* is used to refer to secret key cryptography, and *PKC* is used to refer to public key cryptography. Consequently, an X in the table indicates that the authentication and key distribution system mentioned in the line uses the cryptographic technique mentioned in the column.

Taking the description one step further, we can see that most authentication and key distribution systems use MD4 and MD5 as one-way hash functions, DES as secret key cryptosystem, and RSA as the public key cryptosystem. However, some systems don't follow this general rule of thumb: NetSP uses CDMF instead of DES, and the cipher toolbox of TESS also provides implementations of FEAL and IDEA, as well as a stream cipher based on linear feedback shift registers. With regard to public key cryptography, TESS uses the ElGamal scheme instead of RSA.

Table 8.2
Cryptographic Techniques Used by the Systems

System	OWHF	SKC	PKC
Kerberos	X	X	
NetSP	X	(X)	
SPX	X	X	X
TESS	X	X	X
SESAME	X	X	X
OSF DCE	X	X	X

Nevertheless, it is important to note that any authentication and key distribution system targeted to be used on a large scale should follow a hybrid approach. As a matter of fact, the use of public key cryptography for authentication and key distribution has many advantages. In particular, it makes it possible to significantly increase the efficiency and scalability of an authentication and key distribution system.

Another point that can be used to differentiate the authentication and key distribution systems is the way they protect themselves against replay attacks. In particular, Kerberos, SPX, SESAME, and OSF DCE all use timestamps, whereas TESS uses challenge-response mechanisms. NetSP is in fact the only authentication and key distribution system that supports both possibilities. Remember that we have briefly touched upon the corresponding protocol changes in Chapter 3.

One thing that should be kept in mind, and that we haven't addressed sufficiently so far, is the fact that most cryptographic techniques are covered by patents. With respect to secret key cryptography, DES is patented but royalty free. Similarly, IDEA is patented and royalty free for noncommercial use, but requires a license for commercial use. Most public key cryptosystems are patented, and most of the important patents have been acquired by Public Key Partners (PKP) [1]. As a matter of fact, the MIT and the Board of Trustees of the Leland Stanford Junior University have granted PKP exclusive sublicensing rights to the U.S. patents summarized in Table 8.3 and all of their corresponding foreign patents.

In general, it is the responsibility of the user of a particular cryptographic technique to make sure that the correct license has been obtained from the corresponding patent holder. Consequently, anybody who wants to use SPX, SESAME, or OSF DCE in the United States has to make sure that a corresponding RSA license has been obtained from PKP. Note that the ElGamal signature scheme has not been

Table 8.3
U.S. Patents Held by Public Key Partners (PKP)

Patent #	Authors	Year
4,200,770	Diffie-Hellman	1980
4,218,582	Merkle-Hellman	1980
4,405,829	Rivest-Shamir-Adleman	1983
4,424,414	Hellman-Pohlig	1984

patented in the United States, and that the use of TESS provides some advantages in this respect. Also note that U.S. patents generally expire after 17 years, and that the first patents on public key cryptography, namely the Diffie-Hellman and Merkle-Hellman patents, will expire in 1997.

8.3   STANDARDIZATION

From a user's point of view, an authentication and key distribution system that conforms to international standards has many advanatages and is more attractive than any proprietary system. Table 8.4 shows what authentication and key distribution systems conform to which standards.

Table 8.4
Standards to Which the Systems Conform

System	Standards
Kerberos	RFC 1510, GSS-API
NetSP	GSS-API
SPX	RFC 1507, ITU-T X.509, GSS-API
TESS	RFC 1824
SESAME	ITU-T X.509, GSS-API, ECMA
OSF DCE	GSS-API

With regard to authentication and key distribution in computer networks and distributed systems, the most important standardization work is currently being done within the Internet community. Taking this into account, it is important to note that Kerberos, SPX, and TESS have all been specified in corresponding request for comments (RFCs). In addition to that, all authentication and key distribution systems except TESS provide an application programming interface (API) that conforms to the GSS-API (compare Appendix A). The GSS-API is notably the most important standard an authentication and key distribution system should conform to. It makes it possible to modify network applications to additionally support authentication without eliminating the possibility to move to other systems later on. If these new systems also conform to the GSS-API, then the corresponding network applications don't need to be modified again to support authentication.

In addition to these Internet-related standards, some authentication and key distribution systems additionally conform to ITU-T and ECMA standards. In particular, SPX and SESAME both use certification hierarchies that are closely related to ITU-T recommendation X.509, whereas SESAME is strongly influenced by related ECMA standards, too.

8.4   AVAILABILITY

With respect to the availability of the authentication and key distribution systems, it is important to note that some systems are in the public domain, whereas others are sold by vendors. For some systems there even exist both possibilities. The situation is summarized in Table 8.5. In the table headings, the term *CV* is used to refer to commercial versions of the system, whereas *PD* is used to refer to public domain versions. Consequently, an X in the table indicates that the authentication and key distribution system mentioned in the line is available as commercial or public domain version accordingly.

Table 8.5
Availability of the Systems

System	CV	PD
Kerberos	X	X
NetSP	X	
SPX		X
TESS		
SESAME	X	X
OSF DCE	X	

We have noted in Chapter 2 that MIT has made both reference implementations of Kerberos V4 and V5 publicly available on the Internet. But, in addition to that, some companies who have been involved in the Athena project from the very beginning have also implemented their version of Kerberos. These implementations are being sold today as commercial products.

In Chapter 3, we introduced NetSP as being a commercial product that implements the KK protocols. The product has been developed and is being sold by IBM. Contrary to NetSP, SPX has been introduced as being an authentication and key distribution system designed and prototyped by DEC. The system is publicly and freely available on the Internet today. SESAME is freely available for noncommercial use, and available on license for inclusion in commercial products. OSF DCE is available in commercial products, too. With respect to TESS, the availability of the system has not been clarified yet.

However, it is only fair to mention at this point that commercial versions of authentication and key distribution systems, in general, tend to be coupled with better and more professional support than public domain versions are used to do. This fact should be kept in mind when evaluating an authentication and key distribution system that suits the requirements of a specific environment.

8.5   EXPORTABILITY

In the United States, certain cryptographic systems and technical data regarding them are deemed to be defense articles and are subject to Federal government export controls as specified in Title 22, *Code of Federal Regulations*, Parts 120 – 128. Consequently, if a U.S. company wants to sell cryptographic systems and technical data to other countries, it has to have export approval. Some exports must be licensed by the Offices of Defense Trade Controls and Munitions Control of the *Department of State* (DoS), whereas others must be licensed by the Office of Export Administration of the *Department of Commerce* (DoC). In general, the DoS is responsible for licensing cryptographic systems and technical data that are used for data encryption, whereas the DoC is responsible for licensing cryptographic systems and technical data that are used for authentication and access control as well as proprietary hardware devices and software.

In spite of this general distinction, the export control laws around encryption are not too clear, and their interpretation changes over time [2]. Sometimes companies get so discouraged that they leave encryption out of their products altogether. Sometimes they generate products that, when sold overseas, have encryption mechanisms seriously weakened or even removed. It is usually possible to get export approval for encryption if the key length is reduced. So, sometimes companies just use short keys, or sometimes they have the capability of varying the key length, and they fix the key length to be shorter when a system is sold overseas.

Table 8.6
Exportability of the Systems

System	Exportable
Kerberos	no
NetSP	yes
SPX	no
TESS	—
SESAME	—
OSF DCE	no

The exportability of the authentication and key distribution systems that have been described and discussed in this book are summarized in Table 8.6. Note that both European systems, namely TESS and SESAME, don't have to deal with U.S. export controls. With regard to the U.S. systems, Kerberos, SPX, and OSF DCE are not exportable in their standard forms, whereas NetSP is exportable due to its use of CDMF. With regard to Kerberos and SPX, it should be mentioned that both systems are distributed only to individuals who declare themselves as U.S. citizens working for the United States, and who agree not to disclose information found in the source code to people who are not authorized to access the information. With regard to OSF DCE, it should be mentioned that it is generally easier to enforce export controls for a commercial product than it is for the distribution of public domain software.

REFERENCES

[1] R. Fougner, "Public Key Standards and Licenses," Request for Comments 1170, January 1991.

[2] S. Landau, S. Kent, C. Brooks, S. Charney, D.E. Denning, W. Diffie, A. Lauck, D. Miller, P. Neumann, and D. Sobel, "Codes, Keys and Conflicts: Issues in U.S. Crypto Policy," ACM Press, June 1994.

Chapter 9

Epilog

The TCP/IP communication protocol suite is used in many thousands of networks to interconnect millions of hosts throughout the world, and the resulting internet is commonly referred to as the *Internet*. Today, the Internet is the world's largest computer network and it even continues its triumphant advance. It has doubled in size each year since 1988, and projections based on its current growth rate point to over 1 million computer networks and well over 1 billion users connected by the end of the century. The Internet is commonly seen as the focal point for what is more politically referred to as an information superhighway or national information infrastructure (NII).

Because of its own dynamics, the Internet has already changed significantly. The initial, research-oriented Internet and its protocol suite were designed for a benign environment best described as collegial, where users and hosts were mutually trusting and interested in a free, open exchange of information. These days, the Internet environment is less collegial and trustworthy; it encompasses all the risks, dangerous situations, and human vices found in society as a whole.

The Internet's openness has been both its strength and its point of vulnerability, making it a convenient tool for attacking hosts connected to the Internet. On November 2, 1988, the Internet Worm flooded thousands of hosts [1,2]; since

153

then, reports of attempted and successful system intrusions have grown dramatically. Weaknesses of systems on the Internet leave them open to various types of exploitation.

Today, virtually everyone on the Internet is vulnerable, and security problems generate much fear throughout the computer and communications industries. Concerns about security problems have even begun to chill the overheated expectations about the Internet's readiness for full commercial activity, possibly delaying or preventing its service as a mass medium for the information superhighway or NII. Several studies have independently shown that many individuals and companies are abstaining from joining the Internet simply because of security concerns. At the same time, analysts are warning companies about the dangers of not being connected to the Internet.

In this conflicting situation, almost everyone agrees that the Internet needs more and better security. However, not everyone agrees on what Internet security means and what it should consist of. Besides authentication and key distribution systems, the Internet community is also investigating firewalls, one-time password systems, network-layer security protocols, and secure message-handling systems. There seems to be no single answer to all Internet security problems.

Today, firewall technology is the most widely deployed security technique within the Internet community [3,4]. A firewall refers to an intermediate system positioned between a trusted network and the Internet. The aim is to erect an outer security wall, or perimeter, that prevents unwanted or unauthorized communication into or out of the network, and provides a single choke point for imposing both security and audit. In principle, a firewall provides a static traffic-routing service at the network layer, using screening routers, or at the application level using proxy servers or application layer gateways.

A pair of historical analogies can help us better understand the role of firewall technology for the Internet [5].

- Our Stone Age predecessors lived in caves, each inhabited by a family whose members knew each other quite well. They could use this knowledge to identify and authenticate one another. Someone wanting to enter the cave would have to be introduced by a family member trusted by the others. Human history has shown that this security model is too simple to work on a large scale. As families grew in size and started to interact with one another, it was no longer possible for all family members to know all other members of the community, or even to reliably remember all persons who had ever been introduced to them.

- In the Middle Ages, our predecessors lived in castles and villages surrounded by town walls. The inhabitants were acquainted with each other, but this web of knowledge was not trusted. Instead, identification and authentication, as well as authorization and access control, were centralized at a front gate. Anyone who wanted to enter the castle or village had to pass the front gate and was thoroughly checked there. Those who managed to pass the gate were implicitly trusted by all inhabitants. But human history has shown that this security model doesn't work either. For one thing, town walls don't protect against malicious insider attacks; for another, the use of town walls and front gates doesn't scale easily. Many remnants of medieval town walls bear witness to this lack of scalability.

The Internet has just entered the Middle Ages. The simple security model of the Stone Age still works for single hosts and local area networks. But it no longer works for wide area networks in general and the Internet in particular. As a first (and let's hope intermediate) step, firewalls have been erected at the Internet gateways. Because they are capable of selectively dropping or forwarding IP datagrams, firewalls also restrict the connectivity of the Internet as a whole. The Internet's firewalls are thus comparable to the town walls and front gates of the Middle Ages. Screening routers correspond to general-purpose gates, while proxy servers and application-layer gateways correspond to more specialized gates.

We don't see town walls anymore. Instead, countries issue certificates (passports) to their citizens to use worldwide for identification and authentication. The Internet may need a similar means of security. Trusted third parties could issue globally accepted certificates for Internet participants, and these certificates could be used to provide security services such as authentication, data confidentiality and integrity, access control, and non-repudiation services. Consequently, there are two main challenges related to Internet security:

1. To build a global certification hierarchy;

2. To develop authentication and key distribution systems that make use of this hierarchy.

The authentication and key distribution systems that have been described and discussed in this book may hopefully serve as a starting point and reference to address both of them in the near future.

REFERENCES

[1] J.A. Rochlis and M.W. Eichin, "With Microscope and Tweezers: The Worm from MIT's Perspective," *Communications of the ACM*, Vol. 32, 1989, pp. 689 – 703.

[2] E.H. Spafford, "The Internet Worm: Crisis and Aftermath," *Communications of the ACM*, Vol. 32, 1989, pp. 678 – 688.

[3] W.R. Cheswick, and S.M. Bellovin, *Firewalls and Internet Security: Repelling the Wily Hacker*, Reading, MA: Addison-Wesley, 1994.

[4] D.B. Chapman, and E.D. Zwicky, *Internet Security Firewalls*, Sebastopol, CA: O'Reilly & Associates, Inc., 1995.

[5] R. Oppliger, "Internet Kiosk: Internet security enters the Middle Ages," *IEEE Computer*, Vol. 28, October 1995, pp. 100 – 101.

Appendix A

GSS-API

It is commonly agreed that security services in general, and authentication and key distribution protocols in particular, should be hidden from the network application programmer. Essentially all the programmer should need to know is how to incorporate security services into given applications. Additionally, the programming task would be made easier if there was some standard way of accessing security services so that the application would be portable across platforms and architectures.

The common authentication technology (CAT) working group (WG) of the Internet Engineering Task Force (IETF) was chartered to address these problems, and September 1993, the IETF CAT WG proposed a generic security service application programming interface (GSS-API) in RFC 1508 [1], and corresponding bindings for the C programming language in RFC 1509 [2].

Initially, the GSS-API was intended to provide interoperability between environments that use different authentication and key distribution systems. The aim was to define security services and service primitives in a generic fashion, supportable with a range of underlying security mechanisms and technologies and hence allowing source-level portability of applications to different environments. The GSS-API addresses the following design goals:

157

- *Mechanism independence:* The GSS-API should define an interface to cryptographically implemented strong authentication and other security services at a generic level that is independent of particular underlying mechanisms.

- *Protocol environment independence:* The GSS-API should be independent of the communications protocol suites with which it is employed, permitting use in a broad range of environments.

- *Protocol association independence:* The GSS-API security context construct should be independent of communications protocol association constructs.

- *Suitability to a range of implementation placements:* GSS-API clients should not be constrained to reside within any trusted computing base perimeter defined on a system where the GSS-API is implemented.

The GSS-API version 1 (v1) has been incorporated into most authentication and key distribution systems today, and the IETF CAT WG is currently working on incremental changes in response to implementation experience and liaison requests. The resulting GSS-API version 2 (v2), however, is in progress and not considered as stable [3]. In this appendix we therefore focus on GSS-API v1, and whenever we talk about GSS-API we implicitly refer to GSS-API v1.

In general, the GSS-API operates in the following paradigm: A typical GSS-API caller is itself a communications protocol, calling on GSS-API in order to protect its communications with authentication, integrity, and/or confidentiality services. A GSS-API caller accepts tokens provided to it by its local GSS-API implementation and transfers the tokens to a peer on a remote system. The peer passes the received tokens to its local GSS-API implementation for further processing.

The set of calls offered by the GSS-API can be divided into four groups, and each of these groups is briefly overviewed in one of the following sections.

Credential Management Calls

GSS-API *credential management calls* are related to the acquisition and release of credentials by principals. The available calls are summarized in Table A.1.

- The `GSS_Acquire_cred()` call provides a means to acquire credentials for use by a principal.

- The `GSS_Release_cred()` call provides a means to discard credentials after use by a principal.

Table A.1
GSS-API Credential Management Calls

GSS-API Call	Action
GSS_Acquire_cred()	Acquire credentials
GSS_Release_cred()	Discard credentials
GSS_Inquire_cred()	Determine information about credentials

- The GSS_Inquire_cred() call provides a means to determine information about credentials.

Context-Level Calls

GSS-API *context-level calls* are related to the establishment and management of security contexts between principals. The available calls are summarized in Table A.2.

Table A.2
GSS-API Context-Level Calls

GSS-API Call	Action
GSS_Init_sec_context()	Initiate an outbound security context
GSS_Accept_sec_context()	Accept an inbound security context
GSS_Delete_sec_context()	Discard a security context
GSS_Process_context_token()	Process context control token
GSS_Context_time()	Determine context lifetime

- The GSS_Init_sec_context() call provides a means to initiate an outbound security context with a peer application. In principle, the GSS_Init_sec_context() call generates a token that the caller can send to the target.

- The GSS_Accept_sec_context() call provides a means to accept an inbound security context initiated by a peer application. Depending on the underlying security mechanisms and specified options, additional token exchanges may be performed in the course of a context establishment.

- The GSS_Delete_sec_context() call provides a means to discard a security context, and to release information that is no longer required.

- The GSS_Process_context_token() call provides a means to process tokens on security contexts from peer applications.

- The GSS_Context_time() call provides a means to determine for how long a context will remain valid.

Per-Message Calls

GSS-API *per-message calls* are related to the protection of individual messages on established security contexts. The available calls are summarized in Table A.3. The four members of this group should be considered as two pairs; the output from GSS_Sign() is properly input to GSS_Verify(), and the output from GSS_Seal() is properly input to GSS_Unseal().

Table A.3
GSS-API Per-Message Calls

GSS-API Call	Action
GSS_Sign()	Digitally sign message
GSS_Verify()	Verify digital signature
GSS_Seal()	Seal message
GSS_Unseal()	Unseal message

- The GSS_Sign() call provides a means to digitally sign a message.

- The GSS_Verify() call provides a means to verify a digital signature.

- The GSS_Seal() call provides a means to seal a message.

- The GSS_Unseal() call provides a means to unseal a message.

Support Calls

GSS-API *support calls* provide ancillary functions. The available calls are summarized in Table A.4.

Table A.4
GSS-API Support Calls

GSS-API Call	*Action*
GSS_Display_status()	Convert status codes to text
GSS_Indicate_mechs()	Indicate security mechanism types
GSS_Compare_name()	Compare two internal names
GSS_Display_name()	Convert internal name to text
GSS_Import_name()	Convert text to internal name
GSS_Release_name()	Discard an internal name
GSS_Release_buffer()	Discard a buffer
GSS_Release_oid_set()	Discard a set of object identifiers

- The GSS_Display_status() call provides a means to convert returned status codes into printable string representations, such as text.

- The GSS_Indicate_mechs() call provides a means to determine and indicate the set of mechanism types available on a local system. Note that this call is intended for support of specialized callers who need to request nondefault mechanism type sets from GSS_Acquire_cred(), and should not be used by other callers.

- The GSS_Compare_name() call provides a means to compare two internal name representations for equality.

- The GSS_Display_name() call provides a means to convert an internal name representation into a printable string representation, such as text. In general, the syntax of the printable string representation is a local matter.

- The GSS_Import_name() call makes it possible to provide a printable name representation, such as text, designate the type of namespace in conjunction with which it should be parsed, and convert that printable representation to an internal name suitable for input to other GSS-API calls.

- Three calls, namely GSS_Release_name(), GSS_Release_buffer(), and GSS_Release_oid_set() provide means to discard data objects to release storage.

More recently, an interface for *Secure Network Programming* (SNP) has been designed and prototyped at the University of Texas at Austin. SNP provides a high-level abstraction for secure end-to-end network communications. It is designed to resemble the Berkeley sockets interface so that security can be retrofitted into existing socket programs with only minor modifications. SNP is built on top of GSS-API, thus making it relatively portable across different authentication mechanisms conforming to GSS-API. SNP hides the details of GSS-API, the communication sublayer as well as the cryptographic sublayer from application programmers.

REFERENCES

[1] J. Linn, "Generic Security Service Application Program Interface," Request for Comments 1508, September 1993.

[2] J. Wray, "Generic Security Service API: C-bindings," Request for Comments 1509, September 1993.

[3] J. Linn, "Generic Security Service Application Programming Interface — Version 2," Internet Draft, March 1995, work in progress.

Glossary

Access control The process of preventing of unauthorized use of resources, including the prevention of use of resources in an unauthorized manner.

Accounting The process of measuring resource usage of a particular principal.

Accountability Property that ensures that the actions of a particular principal may be traced uniquely to this principal.

Authentication The process of verifying the claimed identity of a principal.

Authentication context Information conveyed during a particular instance of authentication.

Authentication exchange A sequence of one or more messages sent for authentication.

Authentication information Information used for authentication.

Authentication token Data record that holds authentication information.

Authenticator Data record that contains information that can be shown to have been recently generated using the session key known only by a client and a requested server.

Authorization The process of granting rights, which includes the granting of access based on access rights.

Authorization policy A set of rules, part of an access control policy by which access by subjects to objects is granted or denied. An authorization policy may be defined in terms of access control lists, capabilities, or attributes assigned to subjects, objects or both.

Availability The property of being accessible and usable upon demand by an authorized entity.

Capability Data record that can serve as an identifier for a resource such that possession confers access rights for the resource.

Cell Administration domain in OSF DCE.

Certificate Data record that provides the public key of a principal, together with some other information related to the name of the principal and the certification authority that has issued the certificate. The certificate is rendered unforgeable by appending a digital signature from the certification authority.

Certification authority Trusted third party that creates, assigns, and distributes certificates.

Certification path A sequence of certificates starting with a certificate issued by one principal's certification authority (CA) and ending with a certificate for another principal, where each certificate in the path contains the public key to check the following certificate.

Certification revocation Announcement that a private key has or may have fallen into the wrong hands and that the certificate that belongs to the corresponding public key should no longer be used for authentication.

Ciphertext The output of an encryption function. Encryption transforms plaintext into ciphertext.

Claimant Principal that seeks to be recognized as authentic.

Client A process that requests and eventually obtains a network service. A client is usually acting on a user's behalf.

Communication compromise Result of the subversion of a communication line within a computer network or distributed system.

Computer network Interconnected collection of autonomous computer systems.

Confidentiality The property that information is not made available or disclosed to unauthorized parties.

Credentials Data record that is needed to establish the claimed identity of a principal. In the Kerberos model, credentials refer to a ticket plus the secret session key necessary to successfully use that ticket for authentication.

Cross certifying CA Certification authority (CA) that is trusted to issue certificates for arbitrary principals and CAs over which it may not have immediate jurisdiction.

Cryptology Science of secure communications.

Decipherment The reversal of encipherment.

Delegation The process that one principal allows another principal to act on his behalf.

Delegation key A key that is used for delegation.

Denial of service The prevention of authorized access to resources or the delaying of time-critical operations.

DES Secret key cryptosystem (data encryption standard).

Digital signature Data appended to, or a cryptographic transformation of a data unit that allows a recipient of the data unit to prove the source and integrity of the data unit and to protect against forgery (e.g., by the recipient).

Distributed system Computer network in which the existence of multiple autonomous computer systems is transparent, and thus not necessarily visible to the user.

ECMA The European Computer Manufacturer Association (ECMA) is a European association founded in 1961 dedicated to the standardization of information and communication systems.

Encipherment The cryptographic transformation of data to produce ciphertext.

Host Addressable entity within a computer network or distributed system. The entity is typically addressed either by its name, or by its network layer address.

Host compromise Result of the subversion of an individual host within a computer network or distributed system.

IDEA Secret key cryptosystem (international data encryption algorithm).

Information Knowledge communicated or received concerning a particular fact or circumstance in general, and data that can be coded for processing by a computer or similar device in computer science.

Information technology (IT) Technology that deals with information.

Initiator Principal acting in an active role, for example, requesting access.

Integrity The property of ensuring that data is transmitted from a source to destination without undetected alterations.

Interleaving attack Attack that is based on the attacker's ability to use either legitimate message flows obtained from past executions of a protocol or message flows elicited by the attacker from legitimate parties.

Interrealm authentication Authentication across realm boundaries.

Interrealm key Secret key that is shared between two key distribution centers (KDC) in different Kerberos realms.

ISO The International Organization for Standardization (ISO) is a non-governmental, worldwide federation of national standards bodies established in 1947. The mission of the ISO is to promote the development of standardization and related activities in the world with a view to facilitating the international exchange of goods and services, and to developing cooperation in the spheres of intellectual, scientific, technological and economic activity.

ITU The International Telecommunications Union (ITU) is an international organization within which governments and the private sector coordinate global telecommunications networks and services. ITU activities include the coordination, development, regulation, and standardization of telecommunications.

Kerberos An authentication and key distribution system that has been developed at the MIT.

Key A sequence of symbols that controls the operations of encipherment and decipherment.

Key management The generation, storage, distribution, deletion, archiving and application of keys in accordance with a security policy.

Key pair A set of a public and a private key that belong together.

Label Security-relevant information associated with an object.

Limitation Feature that is not as general as possible.

Masquerade The unauthorized pretense by a principal to be a different principal.

NetSP An authentication and key distribution system that has been developed by IBM (Network Security Program).

Nonce Fresh and unpredictable random number.

Non-repudiation The property of a receiver being able to prove that the sender of some data did in fact send the data even though the sender might later desire to deny ever having sent it.

Open system System that conforms to open system standards.

Open system standard Standard that specifies an open system, and that allows any manufacturer to build corresponding products.

OSF The Open Software Foundation (OSF) was founded in 1988 as a consortium of companies who wanted to cooperate in the development of software for the open systems market.

OSI-RM Preeminent model for structuring and understanding communication functions in computer networks and distributed systems. The reference model for open systems interconnection (OSI-RM) was originally proposed by the ISO/IEC JTC1 in 1978.

Plaintext The input of an encryption function or the output of a decryption function. Decryption transforms ciphertext into plaintext.

Preauthentication Authentication prior to the actual authentication exchange.

Principal Human or system entity that is registered in and authenticatable to a computer network or distributed system.

Principal identifer Identifer used to uniquely identify a principal.

Private key Cryptographic key used in public key cryptography to sign and/or decrypt messages.

Process Instantiation of a program running on a particular host.

Protocol Specification of the format and the relative timing of a finite sequence of messages.

Public key The key used in an asymmetric cryptosystem that is publicly available.

RC2, RC4, and RC5 Secret key cryptosystems.

Realm Authentication domain in Kerberos.

Replay attack An attack on an authentication system by recording and replaying previously sent valid messages or parts thereof. Any constant authentication information, such as a password, a one-way hash of a password, or even electronically transmitted biometric data, can be recorded and used later to forge messages that appear to be authentic.

Repudiation Denial by one of the entities involved in a communication of having participated in all or part of the communication.

RSA Public key cryptosystem (Rivest, Shamir and Adleman).

Secret key The key used in a symmetric cryptosystem that is shared between the communicating parties.

Security architecture A high-level description of the structure of a system, with security functions assigned to components within this structure.

Security attribute A piece of security information which is associated that a principal in a distributed system.

Security audit An independent review and examination of system records and activities in order to test for adequacy of system controls, to ensure compliance with established policy and operational procedures, to detect breaches in security, and to recommend any indicated changes in control, policy, and procedures.

Security audit message A message generated following the occurrence of an auditable security-related event.

Security audit trail Data collected and potentially used to facilitate a security audit.

Self-certified public key Public key that can be computed from its holder's identification and some other public information.

Server Process that provides a network service.

Service Coherent set of abstract functionality.

Session key A temporary key shared between two or more principals, with a limited lifetime.

SESAME An authentication and key distribution system that is being developed as part of a research and development project.

SPX An authentication and key distribution system designed and prototyped by DEC.

Standard A documented agreement containing technical specifications or other precise criteria to be used consistently as rules, guidelines, or definitions of characteristics to ensure that materials, products, processes and services are fit for their purpose.

Target Principal acting in a passive role, for example, being accessed.

TESS A toolbox set system of different but cooperating cryptographic mechanisms and functions based on the primitive of discrete exponentiation.

Threat Circumstance, condition, or event with the potential to either violate security or to cause harm to system resources.

Ticket Data record that can be used for authentication.

Traffic analysis The inference of information from observation of traffic flows (presence, absence, amount, direction, and frequency).

Traffic padding The generation of spurious instances of communication, spurious data units, or spurious data within data units.

Trusted third party A security authority or its agent, trusted by other entities with respect to security-related activities.

User Principal who is to be made accountable and ultimately responsible for his activities within a computer network or distributed system.

Verifier A principal seeking to authenticate a claimant.

Vulnerability A weakness that can be exploited to violate a system or the information that it contains.

Abbreviations and Acronyms

ACL	access control list
AES	application environment specification
ANSI	American National Standards Institute
APA	authentication and privilege attribute
API	application programming interface
AS	authentication server
ASN.1	abstract syntax notation 1
ATM	asynchronous transfer mode
BAN	Burrows, Abadi, and Needham
Bellcore	Bell Communications Research
BER	basic encoding rules
BFI	Swiss Federal Office of Information Technology and Systems
CA	certification authority
CAA	certification authority agent
CAE	common applications environment
CAT	common authentication technology

CBC	cipher block chaining
CCITT	Consultative Committee on International Telegraphy and Telephony (now ITU-T)
CD	compact disk
CDC	certificate distribution center
CDMF	commercial data masking facility
CDS	cell directory service
CEC	Commission of the European Communities
CFB	cipher feedback
CSF	cryptographic support facility
CV	control value
DAC	discretionnary access control
DASS	distributed authentication security service
DCE	distributed computing environment
DEC	Digital Equipment Corporation
DES	data encryption standard
DIT	directory information tree
DNS	domain name service
DoC	U.S. Department of Commerce
DoD	U.S. Department of Defense
DoD	U.S. Department of State
DOS	disk operating system
DSA	digital signature algorithm
DSS	digital signature standard
	domain security server
DSSA	distributed system security srchitecture
DTI	directory information tree
ECB	electronic code book
ECMA	European Computer Manufacturers Association
EDI	electronic data interchange
EES	exponential electronic eignature
EISS	European Institute for System Security
EKE	encrypted key exchange
EPAC	extended privilege attribute certificate
EU	European Union

FAQ	frequently asked questions
FEAL	fast encryption algorithm
FIPS	Federal Information Processing Standard
FTP	file transfer protocol
GDA	global domain agent
GDS	global domain service
GNY	Gong, Needham, and Yahalom
GSS-API	generic security service API
HP	Hewlett-Packard
IAM	Institute for Computer Science and Applied Mathematics
IBM	International Business Machines Corporation
ICL	International Computers Limited
ICSI	International Computer Science Institute
IDEA	international data encryption algorithm
IDS	inter domain service
IEC	International Electrotechnical Committee
IEEE	Institute of Electrical and Electronic Engineers
IETF	Internet Engineering Task Force
IP	internet protocol
IPSEC	IP security protocol
IPST	IP secure tunnel protocol
IS	International Standard
ISO	International Organization for Standardization
ISODE	ISO development environment
IT	information technology
ITU-T	International Telecommunication Union — Telecommunication Standardization Sector
JTC1	Joint Technical Committee 1
KDC	key distribution center
KDS	key distribution server
KEK	key encryption key
KTC	key translation center

LAN	local area network
LEAF	login enrollment agent facility
LLC	logical link control
LRA	local registration authority
MAC	message authentication code
MAN	metropolitan area network
MD	message digest
MDC	modification detection code
MHS	message handling system
MIB	management information base
MIC	message integrity code
MIT	Massachusetts Institute of Technology
MKMP	modular key management protocol
NBS	National Bureau of Standards
NCSC	National Computer Security Center
NCSL	National Computer Systems Laboratory
NetSP	network security program
NII	national information infrastructure
NIST	National Institute of Standards and Technology
NLSP	network layer security protocol
NSA	National Security Agency
OFB	output feedback
OSF	Open Software Foundation
OSI	open systems interconnection
OSI-RM	OSI reference model
PAC	privilege attribute certificate
PAS	privilege attribute server
PC	personal computer
PEM	privacy enhanced mail
PGP	pretty good privacy
PIN	personal identification number
PKCS	public key cryptography standard
PKM	public key management

PKP	Public Key Partners
PPID	primary principal identifier
PT	privilege ticket
PTGT	privilege ticket granting ticket
PV	protection value
PVF	PAC validation facility
RACF	resource access control facility
RFC	request for comment
RFT	request for technology
ROM	read only memory
RPC	remote procedure call
RSA	Rivest, Shamir, and Adleman
SACM	secure association context manager
SELANE	secure local area network environment
SESAME	secure European System for Applications in a Multivendor Environment
SHA	secure hash algorithm
SHS	secure hash standard
SKIA	secure key issuing authority
SLC	secured logon coordinator
SMIB	security management information base
SMS	service management system
SNG	secured network gateway
SNI	Siemens Nixdorf Informationssysteme
SNMP	simple network management protocol
SNP	secure network programming
SPKM	simple public-key GSS-API mechanisms
SSE	Software and Systems Engineering (SSE) Ltd
SSO	single sign-on
TA	trusted authority
TAN	transaction authentication number
TCB	trusted computing base
TCP	transport control protocol
TESS	The Exponential Security System

TGS   ticket granting server
TGT   ticket granting ticket
TLSP   transport layer security protocol
TVP   time-variant parameter

UID   user identification
UUID   universal unique identifier
URL   uniform resource locator
US   user sponsor
U.S.   United States

WG   working group
WWW   World Wide Web

Bibliography

Amoroso, E., *Fundamentals of Computer Security Technology*, Englewood Cliffs, NJ: Prentice-Hall, 1994.

ANSI X9.17, American national standard for financial institution key management (wholesale), Washington, DC, 1985.

Baker, R.H., *Computer Security Handbook*, McGraw-Hill, 1991.

Brassard, G., *Modern Cryptology*, Berlin, Germany: Springer-Verlag, 1988.

Carl-Mitchell, S., and Quaterman, J.S., *Practical Internetworking with TCP/IP and UNIX*, Reading, MA: Addison-Wesley, 1993.

Comer, D., *Internetworking with TCP/IP: Principles, Protocols, and Architecture*, Englewood Cliffs, NJ: Prentice-Hall, 1988.

Davies, D.W., and Price, W.L., *Security for Computer Networks*, Chichester, UK: John Wiley & Sons, Ltd., 1984.

Denning, D.E., *Cryptography and Data Security*, Reading, MA: Addison-Wesley, 1982.

Devargas, M., *Network Security*, Oxford, UK: NCC Blackwell, 1993.

Diffie, W., and Hellman, M.E., New Directions in Cryptography, *IEEE Transactions on Information Theory*, IT-22(6), 1976, pp. 644 – 654.

ElGamal, T., *Cryptography and Logarithms Over Finite Fields*, Ph.D. Thesis, Stanford University, 1984.

ElGamal, T., A Public Key Cryptosystem and a Signature Scheme Based on Discrete Logarithm, *IEEE Transactions on Information Theory*, IT-31(4), 1985, pp. 469 – 472.

Ford, W., *Computer Communications Security — Principles, Standard Protocols and Techniques*, Englewood Cliffs, NJ: Prentice Hall, 1994.

IEEE 802.10c/D10, Standard for Interoperable LAN/MAN Security: Clause 3 — Key Mangement Protocol, September 1995.

ISO/IEC 7498-2, Information Processing Systems — Open Systems Interconnection Reference Model — Part 2: Security Architecture, 1989.

ISO/IEC 9594-8, Information technology — Open Systems Interconnection — The Directory — Part 8: Authentication framework, 1990.

ISO/IEC DIS 10181 Parts 1 to 8, Information technology – Security frameworks in open systems, 1993.

ISO/IEC DIS 10181-3, Information technology – Security frameworks in open systems — Part 3: Access control, 1993.

ITU-T X.509, The Directory — Authentication Framework, November 1987.

ITU X.800, Security Architecture for Open Systems Interconnection for CCITT Applications, 1991.

Kahn, D., *The Codebreakers*, New York, NY: MacMillan, 1967.

Kahn, D., *Sezing the Enigma*, Boston, MA: Houghton Mifflin, 1991.

Kaufman, C., Perlman, R., and Speciner, M., *Network Security: Private Communication in a Public World*, Englewood Cliffs, NJ: Prentice Hall, 1995.

Kent, S.T., Internet Privacy Enhanced Mail. *Communications of the ACM*, 36(8), August 1993, pp. 48 – 60.

Konheim, A.G., *Cryptography: A Primer*, New York, NY: John Wiley & Sons, Ltd., 1981.

Lai, X., *On the Design and Security of Block Ciphers*, Dissertation ETH No. 9752, Swiss Federal Institute of Technology, Zürich, Switzerland, 1992.

Meyer, C.H., and Matias, S.M., *Cryptography: A New Dimension in Computer Data Security*, New York, NY: John Wiley & Sons, Ltd, 1982.

Muftic, S., *Security Mechanisms for Computer Networks*, Chichester, UK: Ellis Horwood, Ltd., 1989.

Muftic, S., Patel, A., Sanders, P., Colon, R., Heijnsdijk, J., and Pulkkinen, U., *Security Architecture for Open Distributed Systems*, Chichester, UK: John Wiley & Sons, Ltd., 1993.

NIST, Data Encryption Standard, FIPS PUB 46, Gaithersburg, MD, originally issued by National Bureau of Standards (NBS) in January 1977.

NIST, Secure Hash Standard (SHS), FIPS PUB 180, Gaithersburg, MD, May 1993.

NIST, Digital Signature Standard (DSS), FIPS PUB 186, Gaithersburg, MD, May 1994.

Piscitello, D., and Chapin, A.L., *Open Systems Networking: TCP/IP and OSI*, Reading, MA: Addison-Wesley, 1993.

Purser, M., *Secure Data Networking*, Norwood, MA: Artech House, 1993.

Rhee, M.Y., *Cryptography and Secure Communications*, McGraw-Hill, 1994.

Rivest, R.L., The MD4 Message-Digest Algorithm, Request for Comments 1320, April 1992.

Rivest, R.L., 1995. The RC5 Encryption Algorithm, *Dr. Dobb's Journal*, January 1995, pp. 146 – 148.

Rivest, R.L., and Dusse, S., The MD5 Message-Digest Algorithm, Request for Comments 1321, April 1992.

Rivest, R.L., Shamir, A., and Adleman, L., A Method for Obtaining Digital Signatures and Public-Key Cryptosystems, *Communications of the ACM*, 21(2), February 1978, pp. 120 – 126.

Schneier, B., *Applied Cryptography: Protocols, Algorithms, and Source Code in C*, New York, NY: John Wiley & Sons, Inc., 1994.

Stallings, W., *Network and Internetwork Security*, Englewood Cliffs, NJ: Prentice-Hall, 1994.

Stinson, D., *Cryptography Theory and Practice*, Boca Raton, FL: CRC Press, 1995.

Tanenbaum, A.S., *Computer Networks*, Englewood Cliffs, NJ: Prentice-Hall, 1988.

Zimmermann, P.R., *The Official PGP User's Guide*, Cambridge, MA: The MIT Press, 1995.

Zimmermann, P.R., *PGP Source Code and Internals*, Cambridge, MA: The MIT Press, 1995.

About the Author

Rolf Oppliger received his M.Sc. and Ph.D. degrees in computer science from the University of Berne, Switzerland, in 1991 and 1993, respectively. He is currently with the Swiss Federal Office of Information Technology and Systems (BFI) and the Institute for Computer Science and Applied Mathematics (IAM) of the University of Berne. His research interests are directed towards computer and network security in general, and the use of cryptographic protocols in computer networks and distributed systems in particular. He is a member of the Swiss Informaticians Society (SI) and its working group on security, as well as the Association for Computing Machinery (ACM). He also serves as a vice-chair of IFIP TC 11/WG 4 on network security.

Index

183

context-level calls, 159
credential management calls, 158
cross certifying CA, 89
cryptographic support facility, 124
cryptology, 14

data confidentiality services, 9
data encryption standard, 15
data integrity mechanisms, 11
data integrity services, 9
data origin authentication service, 9
DCE authentication service, 137
DCE authorization, 138
DCE client host, 134
DCE Directory Service, 135
DCE distributed time service, 135
DCE product listing, 132
DCE security service, 136
DCE server host, 134
DCE Threads, 134
delegation, 87
Department of Commerce, 150
Department of State, 150
dialogue key, 125
Diffie-Hellman key exchange, 102
Digital Equipment Corporation, 85, 132
digital signature mechanisms, 11
digital signature scheme, 17
digital signature standard, 17, 102
directory information tree, 24
directory service, 133
discrete exponentiation, 101, 102
discrete logarithm, 101
discretionnary access control, 139
distributed authentication security service, 85
distributed computing environment, 132
distributed file service, 134
distributed system, 2
distributed system security architecture, 85
distributed time service, 133
domain name service, 135
domain security server, 121

ECMA-style privilege attribute service, 119
electronic commerce, 10

electronic data interchange, 10
ElGamal signature scheme, 102
encipherment, 11
European Computer Manufacturer Association, 116
European Institute for System Security, 103
event detection, 13
Exponential Electronic Signature, 106
extended Kerberos V5 authentication service, 119

fast encryption algorithm, 15
foreign group UUIDs, 139

generic security service application programming interface, 157
global directory agent, 135
global directory service, 135

hacker, 5
Hewlett-Packard, 132
host, 3
host compromise, 5

ICEBox, 104
ICECard, 104
information, 1
information superhighway, 153
information technology, 2
initiator, 119
initiator SACM, 124
Institute of Electrical and Electronic Engineers, 21
inter domain service, 124
interleaving attack, 65
International Business Machines, 132
International Computers Ltd, 118
international data encryption algorithm, 15
International Electrotechnical Committee, 3
International Organization for Standardization, 3
International Telecommunication Union, 4
Internet, 153
Internet Engineering Task Force, 37, 157
interrealm authentication, 55
interrealm key, 55